THE JEWISH
ODYSSEY

Translated from the French by Charles Penwarden
Photo Research: Sophie Jaulmes and Eugénie de Paillette
Design: Gwenäel Le Cossec
Copyediting: Chrisoula Petridis
Typesetting: Thierry Renard
Proofreading: Helen Woodhall
Color Separation: Reproscan, Bergamo
Printed in Spain by Grafos

Distributed in North America by Rizzoli International Publications, Inc.

Simultaneously published in French as *Histoires du peuple juif*
© Flammarion, S.A., Paris, 2010

English-language edition
© Flammarion, S.A., Paris, 2010

87, quai Panhard et Levassor
75647 Paris Cedex 13

editions.flammarion.com

10 11 12   3 2 1

ISBN: 978-2-08-030155-0

Dépôt légal: 09/2010

Marek Halter

THE JEWISH
ODYSSEY
An Illustrated History

Flammarion

Two couples.
Between them lie
four thousand years,
and yet they look the same:
same expression,
same gesture.

This image of a Sumerian couple reminds me of my grandparents in Warsaw.

Every Jew, whether from East or West, can identify with it.

Between these two images is the odyssey of the Jewish People.

My odyssey.

Page 8:
*Sumero-Akkadian sculpture
(Iraq Museum, Baghdad).*

Page 9:
*Couple of beggars from
Russian Poland (1930, Vienna).*

*In homage to my parents,
my mother, Perl Halter, a Yiddish poet,
and my father, Salomon Halter, a printer
son of printers, grandson of printers,
great grandson of printers,
and so on for generations,
for having given me the taste for words.*

INTRODUCTION

On my fourth birthday, my grandfather Abraham brought me a gift: wrapped up in an old Yiddish newspaper were two illustrated books for children, *Biblical Tales* and an abridged version of *The Three Musketeers* by Alexandre Dumas.

Warsaw was under Nazi occupation. We had no electricity. I read the two books by candlelight, from cover to cover. Did that nocturnal reading shape my destiny? I don't know. But one thing I am sure of: it saved my life.

We had the good luck, my parents and I, to be able to leave Warsaw before the outbreak of the Germano-Soviet war, thanks to two friends of my father, two Polish Catholics: Righteous people. We traveled through eastern Poland, which was occupied by the Red Army, then Ukraine. Finally, we reached Moscow. There, my mother gave birth to my little sister. But now, once again, the bombs were falling. The Germans were advancing on Moscow. Stalin sent us to Novouzensk, near the Volga, then to Kokand, in faraway Uzbekistan, already crowded by over a million refugees.

Famine, dysentery, and typhus were cutting swathes through this human forest. In the street, skeletal, ghostly figures staggered, groaned and fell. The young Uzbeks patrolling the lower town picked them up, piled their bodies onto the two wheeled-carts called *arbas*, and dumped them in mass graves dug in the desert.

My parents were in the hospital. I was on my own with my little sister. Her name was Berenice, Bousia. Our neighbors advised me to put her into a children's home, and so I did. She died there—of hunger, I am told.

One day, my parents' doctor called me in.

"If you want to save them, you must find some rice."

There were no antibiotics in the Soviet Union in those days. Rice, though, could be found on the black market. How was a little boy to get hold of some? By stealing. The Uzbeks transported their rice harvest in bags strapped to the sides of mules. All you had to do was walk beside them with a knife, slit the bag, and fill your cap with the grains that spilled out. You then took

to your heels to escape their fury. I wasn't fast enough. The Uzbeks always caught me in the end.

One afternoon, when two men were beating me up for taking their rice, I was freed by a gang of thieves. *Real* thieves.

"What's going on?" asked the oldest, a boy of about fifteen.

I explained.

"Well if you can't steal, what can you do?"

"Tell stories."

Why did I talk to him about stories? Perhaps because of those wonderful *Biblical Tales*. That night, in the Kalvak, a piece of waste ground where the ruffians who terrorized the city came together to share out their spoils, I took my first steps as a storyteller.

I started with *The Three Musketeers*. It must have been the characters' tight-knit sense of solidarity—"One for all and all for one"—that appealed to them. When I reached the end of the story, I realized that my new friends were not moving. And so I continued with *Twenty Years After* and *The Vicomte de Bragelonne*. And since the gang still wasn't moving, I made up D'Artagnan's adventures in Jerusalem.

By early morning I had become "Marek who tells stories." We shared out the tasks. They stole by day and gave me my share to help my parents. I spent my days in the municipal library and in the evening I shared with them what I had read. Most of my stories were inspired by the adventures of the Jewish People, or what I knew of them.

And my comrades always wanted more. Unlike so many men of learning, they grasped the importance of Job's words: "For we children of yesterday, we know nothing." I, on the other hand, had just discovered that my story could be other people's story, too. And since knowledge is nothing if it is not shared, I have been continuing with this most eventful story all these years, from one book to the next.

Could the stories in this *Jewish Odyssey*, which reach back four millennia, be a culmination of those tales that, as a very young boy, I shared in Kokand, on the border with Afghanistan? Back then, they fascinated the Uzbek thieves. Perhaps, now, there is a chance that they will not leave my present readers indifferent.

From Sumer to Jerusalem

The Origins of a People

Our story begins in the place where the Bible locates Paradise, in Mesopotamia, between two rivers, the Tigris and the Euphrates. In that valley, four thousand years ago, the Sumerian Empire built the world's first cities with their ziggurats, tiered temples over two hundred feet high. Agriculture flourished and there was a remarkable irrigation system. They built many paths and roads and invented bills of exchange—clay tablets that have since been discovered in their tens of thousand, (and of which the Louvre has large quantities). Their merchants thus traded far beyond the frontiers of the Empire.

But the most important and most revolutionary invention, the one that changed the human condition and founded modern civilization, was cuneiform writing. Without the first abstract alphabet, history would never have known monotheism. For how could men have conveyed the idea of the One God, of an abstraction, using images or pictograms that would, by their very nature, have made Him visible? The invention of writing and that of a single God go hand in hand. They mark the origin of our adventure.

Right:
Economic tablet: inventory of sheep and goats for sacrifice (c. 3000 BCE, Musée du Louvre, Paris).

Without the cuneiform alphabet, the first abstract alphabet in human history, there would have been no One God, no abstract God. For how, five thousand years ago, could man have described an abstraction with pictograms? The abstract God would have immediately become an idol. Is it a coincidence that Abraham was born in Ur, Mesopotamia, in the very place where the cuneiform alphabet was invented? Is it a coincidence that the history of the Jewish People is so closely bound up with that of writing?

Facing page:
Fra Angelico, Holy Trinity altarpiece, The City of Jerusalem (c. 1435, Museo di San Marco, Florence).

God chose two dwellings: the first, Jerusalem, the city that all men look to; the second, writing, in the book that men take with them when the city itself becomes out of reach.

Peopled by Indo-Europeans, the rich Sumerian cities of Ur, Harran, Nineveh, and Mari attracted the poorer Semitic tribes looking for a place to live and work. Around the cities, now fortified against the waves of migrants, great suburbs grew up.

Among these newcomers one tribe stands out, that of a man named Terah. Like all the others, they were Semites. They may have been part of a bigger group, the Amorites, later known as the Aramaeans. They were called the Terahites or the Ivrim, in memory of their ancestor Eber, great-grandson of Shem, or simply because they came from beyond the river—*ever-hanahar* in Hebrew. In short, they "carried the history forward."

Terah settled in the suburb of Ur as a maker of idols. Sumerian society was polytheist. Each god, whether of rain, the sun, fertility, love, or war, was represented in the form of a statuette the size of which depended on the circumstances and what the buyer could afford. Idol makers prospered.

TERAH, A MAKER OF IDOLS IN UR

bram, Terah's youngest son, used to watch his father working. He saw him modeling the clay, covering it with colors, firing it in the kiln. Then he saw him negotiate the price of the figurines with buyers from the city. Sometimes clients opened up and told the maker of idols about their misfortunes and asked his advice: which god would be best for curing a child struck down by fever or saving a field of wheat attacked by locusts? Sometimes, the visitor did not have enough money for an idol and left empty-handed. It was unjust, thought Abram. He began dreaming of a God who would be the same for all, accessible to all, a God who could not be represented, made, sold, or bought. This God would have to be invisible, and therefore abstract. It all seemed so clear. But how should he express it?

It was then that he met Sarai. Sarai means "young princess" in Sumerian. She was born in the city. She was educated and could write. She gave him the answer.

In the suburb of Ur, the situation of his father, Terah, was deteriorating. There were more and more makers of idols, and the growing supply was driving down prices. Large numbers of new immigrants were exhausting the pastureland. The Terahites did not know where to graze their flocks. Terah decided to leave.

Traveling along the riverbanks with his people, he came to Harran, a port city on the Euphrates. There he set up his workshop, as it had been in Ur. But Abram had had enough of idols. One day, in a rage, he smashed the clay effigies made by his father. Not one of them protested; the sky did not grow dark, nor did the earth shake. The lesson was clear: these gods of clay were not true gods. Terah was furious and disowned his son.

ABRAM DREAMS
OF A GOD
WHO IS THE SAME
FOR ALL

SARAI,
AN EDUCATED
YOUNG
CITY-DWELLER

ABRAM
SMASHES
THE IDOLS

Facing page:
Joseph ben David Leipnik, The Destruction of Idols *(1740, British Library, London).*

Right:
Al-Biruni, Abraham Destroys the Idols of the Sabians (The Chronology of the Ancient Nations, 1307, Edinburgh University Library).

"Every man who fights idolatry," says the Talmud, "is a Jew." This rejection of all forms of deification, be it that of a statue, a man, or an idea, is the source of my Jewishness.

The day after this drama, Abram the iconoclast heard a voice. Was this the invisible God he had dreamed of? The voice ordered him to leave his father and Harran and to head south with Sarai and her family, toward a land by the name of Canaan. However, before this break, he and Sarai had to change their name. From now on he would be called *Abraham*, "father of many nations," and Sarai, *Sarah*. New names, new destinies.

In doing as God had told him and crossing the river with Sarah, his nephew Lot, and a part of his father's tribe—those who chose to follow him—did Abraham know that he was initiating a new epoch in human history? His wanderings would lead to the birth of a new people, the Hebrews, who, through his grandson Jacob, would become the people of Israel.

ABRAM HEARS
A VOICE AND
BECOMES
ABRAHAM

Facing page:
Josef Molnar, The Departure
of Abraham *(1850, National
Gallery, Budapest).*

*In leaving Haran for the
land of Canaan Abraham
turned his tribe into bringers
of both objects and ideas.*

Right:
Rembrandt, Abraham
Casting Out Hagar and
Ishmael *(1637, Dutuit
Collection, Musée du
Petit Palais, Paris).*

*By driving out Hagar
the Egyptian and her son
Ishmael nearly four thousand
years ago, Abraham had
no idea that he was sowing
the seeds of the Israelo–
Palestinian conflict.*

I first discovered this history of the Jewish people, which is also my own history, in a little illustrated book for children: *Biblical Tales*. My grandfather gave it to me for my fourth birthday. This was in Warsaw, under the Nazi occupation.

Many times after that I wondered what Abraham looked like. I imagined him with the features of my grandfather. He, too, was called Abraham. He worked at the printing press of a Yiddish newspaper. I was right. When I came to Paris, I discovered the Sumerian statuettes from the Abrahamic period at the Louvre. I couldn't hold back a cry of surprise: they looked so much like the Jews of my childhood, like olives from the same tree. Just like them, these men of Sumer had beards and curls. Their hands were joined, as if they were rubbing them together, repeating a familiar gesture. One statuette represents a couple holding hands. The woman is clearly wearing a headdress like the ones worn by practicing Jewish women today. It is an accurate image of my grandparents and perhaps, too, the image of the grandparents of nearly all the Jews in the world. We are a long way from those other statuettes that have come down to us from Egypt, those men with square shoulders and their arms at their sides!

During the long trek that took them through today's Syria and Golan all the way to the land of Canaan, the tribe of Abraham and their flocks did not go unnoticed. Abraham and his people reached the gates of the fortified city of Salem, today's Jerusalem. The king, Melchizedek, a just king, came to greet them with bread and wine. He blessed Abraham in the name of God Most High. How did this king know of this One God, having only just met the man who first conceived of Him? Thanks to those tablets of engraved clay that messengers carried all around the region, news traveled fast.

THE TOMB
OF THE PATRIARCHS
AND THE "WELL
OF THE SEVEN"

The land of Canaan took its name from *kinahu*, or crimson, referring to the deep, purplish dye that was produced there in workshops by the sea. It was home to many peoples. Rejecting the usual behavior of this violent age, Abraham did not try to drive them out so as to take their place. He stopped in the valley of Mamre, near Hebron. He negotiated with the Hittite Ephron to purchase land and a cave, the cave of Machpelah, which would become the family burial site, the Tomb of the Patriarchs. Later, in the Negev, a region that in those days was fertile and inhabited, he similarly refused to make war on the Philistines. He signed a non-aggression pact with the king, Abimelech. The agreement was reached near a well and sealed by the sacrifice of seven sheep. They called the place Beersheba, the "well of the seven."

Left:
Dirk Bouts the Elder,
Abraham and Melchizedek
(*fifteenth century, Holy
Sacrament altarpiece, church
of Saint Peter, Louvain*).

*The Righteous King
Melchizedek reigned over
the city of Salem, soon to
become Jerusalem. But where
did this polytheist get the
idea of blessing Abraham
the monotheist in the name
of God Most High?*

Facing page:
Jan Provost, Abraham,
Sarah and the Angel
(*sixteenth century, Musée
du Louvre, Paris*).

*The annunciation of Isaac's
birth to Sarah marks
the beginning of what we
call linear history. After
Abraham came Isaac, after
Isaac, Jacob, and so on,
through to the present.*

The Bible tells us that Abraham lived to the age of 175. His son Isaac was born late, for Sarah was infertile. When, at the age of 90, she learned that she was going to be a mother, she burst out laughing. Hence the given name Isaac, or Itzhak: "he shall laugh" in Hebrew. Isaac lived for 180 years. Jacob, his son, died at the age of 147. We are amused by the ages of these patriarchs, but the men who compiled these biblical texts were trying to make the point that this formative period of the Jewish people, who certainly had many different chiefs, was deeply marked by three of them. This era spans over five centuries.

With the filial bond between these three key figures, Abraham, Isaac, and Jacob, the writers of the Bible introduced linear time into history. This was a first, a revolutionary invention in a world that believed in cyclical history. It was now that men began to conceive of historical narrative as we still do today: one generation after another.

SARAH LAUGHS, THE BIRTH OF ISAAC

THE INVENTION OF LINEAR TIME

Below:
Abraham Sacrificing
Isaac *(sixteenth century,
Hebrew Pentateuch,
British Library, London).*

*This word "sacrifice" is
a bad translation. Isaac was not
sacrificed. Does not this event
represent, rather, the first time
God put man to the test?*

Facing page:
*Biblical genealogy: the third age of
the world, from Abraham to David.
Miniatures: busts of Jacob and Lea.*
Illumination by Stephanus Garsia,
Commentary on the Apocalypse, *or*
Beatus de Saint-Sever *(1060 or 1070).*

*It is because man discovered
linear history that he was able
to conceive of the family tree.*

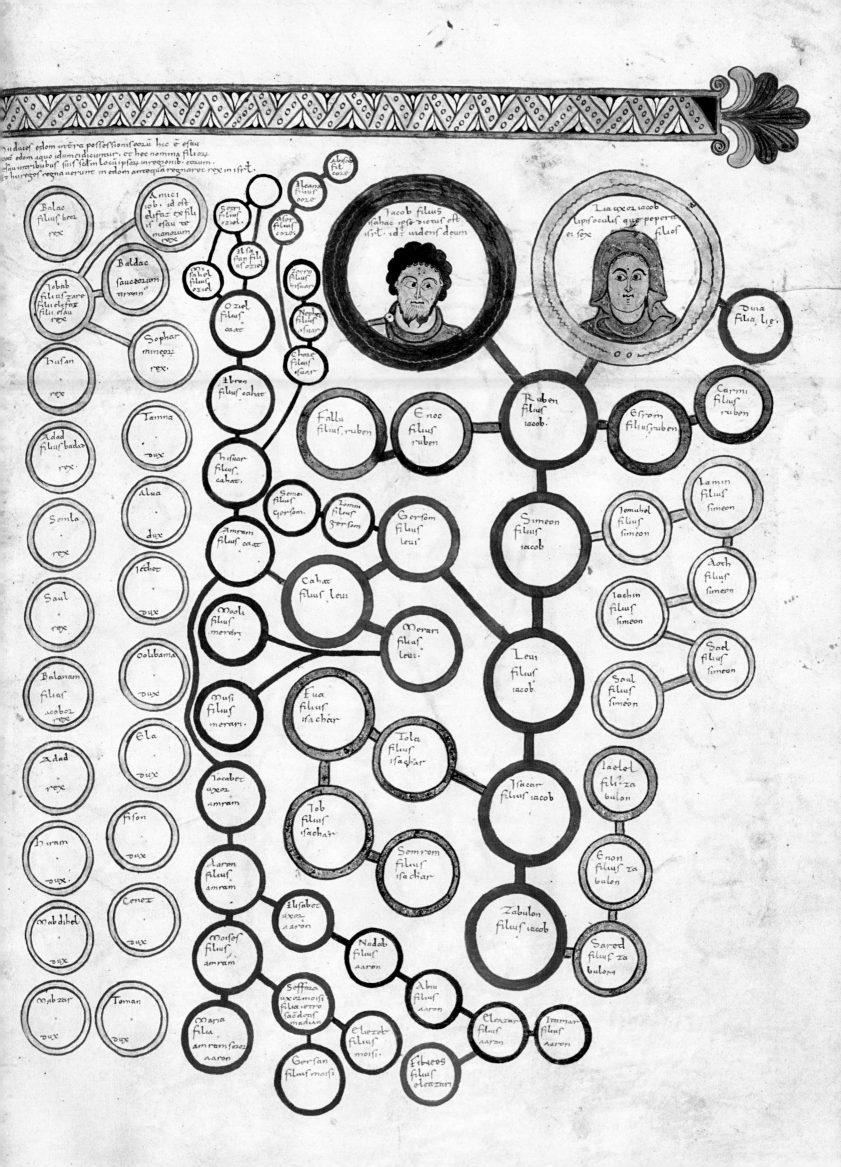

In duces edom intra possessionis eozu hic e esau
uoce edom aquo idumei dicuntur. et hec nomina filioz
esau uxoribus suis sctm locum ipsoz in regionib. eozum
et hu reges regnauerint in edom antequam regnaret rex in isrt.

Balac filius beor rex

Amuci iob. id est elisaz ex filii isf esau te manozum rex

Absab fit eoze

Aleana filius oozo

Seoru filius oziel

Alor filius eoze

Iobab filius zare filius elefas filii esau rex

Baldac sauceozum arran

Or fahel filius oziel

Elsa fan filius oziel

Zeero filius hisuar

husan rex

Sophar mineoz rex

Oziel filius caat

Nopheg filius suar

Adad filius badad rex

Tamna dux

Choze filius suar

Semla rex

Alua dux

Ebron filius caat

Fallu filius ruben

Enoc filius ruben

Ruben filius iacob.

Esrom filius ruben

Carmi filius ruben

Saul rex

Jethet dux

hisuar filius caat.

Lamin filius simeon

Balanam filius iacoboz rex

Oolibama dux

Amram filius caat

Semei filius gerson.

Lomni filius gerson

Gersom filius leui

Simeon filius iacob

Jemuhel filius simeon

Iachin filius simeon

Aoth filius simeon

Adad rex

Ela dux

Mooli filius merari

Cahat filius leui

Merari filius leui.

Leui filius iacob

Soul filius simeon

Sael filius simeon

hiram dux

Fison dux

Musi filius merari.

Eua filius isachar

Tola filius isachar

Isacar filius iacob

Iaelel filii za bulon

Mabdihel dux

Cenez dux

Iocabet uxoz amram

Job filius isachar

Semrom filius isachiar

Enon filius za bulon

Mabzar dux

Teman dux

Aaron filius amram

Elisabet uxoz aaron

Nadab filius aaron

Zabulon filius iacob

Sared filius za bulon

Moises filius amram

Abiu filius aaron

Maria filia amram soroz aaron

Seffoza uxoz moisi filia ietro sacdoas madian

Eleozel filius moisi

Eleazar filius aaron

Itamar filius aaron

Gersan filius moisi

Finees filius eleazan

Jacob filius isahac ipso dictus est isrt. id: uidens deum

Lia uxoz iacob lipis oculis que peperit ei sex filios

Dina filia lie.

JACOB
WRESTLES
WITH AN ANGEL
AND BECOMES
ISRAEL

Jacob, the third and last patriarch, completed the founding myth. He went to seek a wife in Mesopotamia, among the Terahites who had stayed there, just as nowadays many newly naturalized immigrants return to the land of their origins to marry. On the journey back, he saw himself wrestling with a figure—a man or an angel. The fight lasted all night. Jacob emerged victorious. Like Abraham, he changed his name and took that of Israel, which means "God's wrestler" or "one who wrestles with God" in Hebrew. His twelve sons went on to found the twelve tribes that make up the Jewish people, the twelve tribes of Israel.

Today, there are many historians who question the very existence of these figures. It is true that we have no proof. However, we do know a great deal about their world. Extensive archaeological excavation and the hundreds of tablets found and deciphered provide some surprising details that on many counts corroborate the Bible story.

An unusually long drought, and the famine that followed, momentarily interrupted the history of the Hebrews in the land of Canaan. This chapter in the story of the Jewish people begins with a family quarrel. Joseph was Jacob's favorite son, and his brothers were jealous. In order to be rid of him, they decided to sell him to a caravan that was bound for Egypt. Potiphar, an officer in the service of Pharaoh, bought Joseph. Potiphar's wife fell in love with this new slave, but Joseph repelled her advances. She accused him of trying to rape her. And so Joseph was thrown in jail.

Pharaoh's cupbearer, who was visiting the jail, discovered that the Hebrew was adept at interpreting dreams. In those days, dreams were seen as messages sent by the gods. When informed of this, Pharaoh had Joseph brought to his palace. He would not regret it: the young Hebrew easily solved most of his enigmas. A few years later, Joseph was made chancellor. Soon, Jacob's tribe came to Egypt, driven abroad by famine. Joseph forgave his brothers and settled them in a region that was particularly fertile, Goshen.

JOSEPH
IN EGYPT

Some historians date this event to the era of Ramses II, that is to say, 1300 BCE; others put it two centuries before that, in the time of Thutmose III. The first hypothesis invokes the frescoes and bas-reliefs from the time of Ramses II showing slaves building pyramids under the whip of Egyptian taskmasters. The Hebrew slaves mentioned in the Bible immediately come to mind. They also refer to the Merneptah Stela, on which this son of Ramses II, who set out for the land of Canaan to quell the revolt of several kings there, mentions all the peoples he has subdued, adding: "Israel is destroyed. Its seed is no more."

But this last argument can be turned against the upholders of the Ramses II thesis. For if Israel was already in the land of Canaan, then it was no longer in Egypt. However, if these events date from the period of Thutmose III, two centuries earlier, then that would give the Hebrews time to leave Egypt, cross the desert, receive the Ten Commandments, and conquer their new country, a process that took over a century. In 1887 Bedouins at Tell el-Amarna chanced upon some clay tablets that belonged to the archives of the foreign affairs department. These speak of the Habiru (our Hebrews?) entering the land of Canaan en masse. It would therefore be logical that, upon arriving there, Merneptah, Ramses II's general, should have found Israel solidly established.

discovered Moses in the Haggadah. The Haggadah is the text we read on the eve of Passover, the feast that commemorates the liberation of the Hebrews from the tyranny of the pharaohs. Years later, in a little church in Rome, I saw him hewn from stone by Michelangelo's hammer.

He is the first founder of the Jewish people whose age did not reach a mythical figure. Kafka wrote some very tender, sad words that perfectly sum up what we feel about his story: "Moses fails to enter Canaan not because his life is too short but because it is a human life."

Michelangelo, Moses (1513–16, San Pietro in Vincoli, Rome).

Moses as I have imagined him ever since childhood, immortalized in marble centuries ago by Michelangelo.

Moses was born in Egypt, under the reign of Thutmose III—or so I believe. Inscriptions made in the fifteenth century BCE at Serabit el-Khadem, in the middle of the Sinai Mountains, relate the history of a rebel who could well be Moses.

Two centuries lie between Joseph's arrival in Egypt and the birth of the man who would be the lawgiver of the Jewish people. In Joseph's day, Egypt was dominated by the Hyksos. A Semitic people, cousins of the Hebrews, they, too, came from Mesopotamia. But the pharaohs of the Theban dynasty drove out the Hyksos and enslaved the Hebrews, who up to that point had been protected. Worse, for fear of seeing Jacob's descendants multiply and form the majority in the land, they decided to kill all the newborn Jewish boys (Exodus 1:22). According to tradition, in order to save her baby from death, Moses' mother placed him in a papyrus basket and abandoned him to the waters of the Nile. Hatshepsut, the daughter of Pharaoh Thutmose I, later to be the Egypt's only ever queen and pharaoh, found the basket in the rushes. Having no child herself, and moved by this doomed infant, she decided to adopt him. The boy was given the name Moses, the Egyptian for "saved from the waters."

As the adopted son of Pharaoh's daughter, Moses grew up at court. He was quite naturally seen as the cousin of the child who would one day succeed Pharaoh. Only much later did he discover the existence of the Hebrew slaves. One day, on seeing a taskmaster violently whipping one of them, he snatched the whip from the Egyptian's hands and killed him. He ran away and ventured into the Sinai Desert. There, he met a young woman near a well. This was Zipporah, a black woman who was the daughter of Jethro, priest of Midian. She welcomed him into her house and later became his wife. Their first son was called Gershom, which in Hebrew means "stranger here," or, more exactly, "I am an alien in a foreign land."

This name came to symbolize a situation that the Jews would never forget. Leviticus says, "You shall treat the stranger who sojourns with you as the native among you, and you shall love him as yourself,

Facing page:
Workshop of Raphael,
Moses Saved from the
Water *(1518–19, Vatican).*

*What I love about this
picture is not so much the
infant Moses as the wonder
in the eyes of those who
saved him. The Righteous?*

Right:
The Hebrews build cities
for Pharaoh, *Barcelona
Haggadah (c. 1350, British
Library, London).*

*"We were slaves in Egypt."
Back in the Warsaw Ghetto,
I heard this story time and
time again at Passover.
An edifying reminder.*

for you were strangers in the land of Egypt." This rule of solidarity, which is still invoked today—a sign that it is rarely obeyed—is the foundation of all human relations. Already, nearly 3,500 years ago, it appears as one of the first laws of Judaism.

Moses could not forget his persecuted brothers. Zipporah was constantly reminding him of them. Nor could he forget the voice, which was always present, of the One who spoke to Abraham before him. However, Moses proved much less docile than his ancestor. He grew up in a more hierarchical, more realistic and pragmatic civilization than that of Mesopotamia. Further, he was a sedentary man. He knew nothing of the heightened imagination of the nomads, of those traveling peoples for whom life is an adventure, and that chance is constantly putting to the test. For Abraham there was nothing extraordinary about hearing a voice from the sky. For Moses, it was a mirage, an irrational event and therefore suspect.

Moses wanted to know with whom he was dealing. He wanted to know the name of He who was talking. The strange proof provided by the Eternal, the bush which blazed before his eyes yet was not consumed, did not suffice. Moses insisted on knowing his name so that he could tell it to the Hebrews that he was going to free. The answer was prodigious: "I am he who is." This could be freely translated as, "My name is without a name." This answer reveals the specificity, mystery, and power of the God of Israel: he exists independently of our gaze and our grasp. He quite simply *is*.

What happened next is well known. But we do not know how many people followed Moses into the desert. According to the Bible, there were 601,703 men! This figure does not include women or children, who for a start would triple it, at the very least. Nor does it take into account the Egyptian, Libyan, and Syrian slaves and all the others who, on the occasion of any great exodus, take the opportunity to escape from their masters, not to mention Jethro's people, the Midianites who also, joined this fabulous human cohort. It must have been over three million people, with their flocks, their clothes, their food, and their great hope who reached Ramses, a city in the east of the Nile Delta, in the far north of Egypt. Three million souls, out of a population that, in the whole of the Middle East, numbered about four times that, put their trust in the word of Moses and followed him into the desert on the road to Canaan.

William Blake, Moses and the Burning Bush *(1798, Victoria and Albert Museum, London).*

It is difficult, if not impossible, to paint an abstract God. For the Jews as for the Muslims, figurative painting is idolatry. That is why the Jews, an eminently creative people, came so late to the visual arts. It is also why so few Jewish artists are represented in the illustrations to my text. Still, the Bible was an inexhaustible source of subjects for countless artists, like William Blake here.

The Bible tells us that Moses spent forty days on the top of Mount
Sinai, at an altitude of seven thousand five hundred feet. There, he
engraved the Ten Commandments on two stone tablets. They were
later known as the Decalogue, from the Greek *deka logoi*, or "ten
words." Having accomplished this task, Moses came up against his
first obstacle: the inability of the former slaves to be truly free. Upon
coming down from the mountain with the Ten Commandments, he
found his people in a state of frenzy, worshipping the Golden Calf
with libations and wild dances. The unbowed people of yesteryear
were already prepared to submit to the first despot who would promise
them a comfortable and easily obtained future. What was freedom to
them if it meant merely anxiety, a useless ordeal whose purpose they
could not grasp? Was it not better to remain under the lash? Moses
was filled with a terrible rage: he shattered the Tablets of the Law.

Facing page:
Isidor Kaufmann, Friday
Evening *(c. 1920, The Jewish
Museum, New York).*

*The Sabbath, the weekly day
of rest for all (including the
women of the house). In my
childhood memories, it was
above all a day of peace. Even
the poorest families found a
clean cloth to cover the table
when they lit the candles. The
men combed their beards and,
with dignified steps, made
their way to the synagogue.*

Right:
Lodovico Carracci, Moses
Shatters the Tablets of the
Law *(sixteenth century,
Uffizi Gallery, Florence).*

*How I understand Moses'
anger at these men
who preferred slavery to
freedom, however difficult!*

Chance has no place in this unique book: the story uses only scenes that are indispensable. For a long time I wondered why it was that Moses had to inscribe the Tablets a second time. After all, he could easily have been angered without having to shatter the sacred stones. The texts of the two versions of the Law seem at first glance to be identical. But not quite. A small detail of capital importance supplies the answer to my question. It concerns the commandment regarding the keeping of the Sabbath. In the first version, the one in Exodus, in order to institute this special day when no work is allowed, Moses refers to the rest that God allowed himself after creating the world in six days. In the second, in Deuteronomy, he evokes the memory of slavery in Egypt. In a sense, one could say that if the first version of the Ten Commandments is God's version, then the second is humanity's. The Law was dictated out of love for man and not out of love and submission to a god, even if this was the Eternal One.

Moses died at the age of 120 on Mount Nebo, looking out over the Promised Land beyond the Jordan. According to the logic of Judaism, the anonymity of his death is perfect. No one knows where his tomb lies. Thus the temptation of a cult and its attendant idolatry is avoided.

After Moses' death, the Hebrews settled, finally, in the land of Canaan. The rule of law was established and the Judges exercised power. Then, in around 1025 BCE, a major event shook the Jewish society of the day—a society which, up to that point, had managed itself. All the other peoples of the region had their king: now the Hebrews wanted one of their own. They came to Rama, says the Bible, to the last of the Judges, who was Samuel. And they said to him: "Look, you are old, and your sons are not following your example. So give us a king to judge us, like the other nations." Samuel prayed to the Lord and He replied: "Obey the voice of the people in all that they say to you … only, you must give them a solemn warning, and must tell them what the king who will reign over them will do." And so Samuel spoke to the people. It is one of the finest political speeches I have ever read:

> The king will take your sons and direct them to his chariotry and cavalry, and they will run in front of his chariot.
> He will make them plough his fields and gather in his harvest and make his weapons of war and the gear for his chariots. He will take your daughters as perfumers, cooks, and bakers. He will take the best of your fields, your vineyards, and your olive groves and give them to his officials. He will tithe your flocks. … He will take the best of your servants … and make them work for him … and you yourselves will become his slaves.

This is one of the greatest biblical demonstrations of freedom and democracy. Since, despite Samuel's arguments, the people continued to insist, the Judge did their bidding. He gave the Hebrews the king they were calling for—Saul was his name—but at the same time he established what we would call checks and balances: the people were to have their own spokesmen, the prophets.

As long as the kings listened to the prophets, and as long as the priests kept to the spiritual sphere, the Hebrew kingdom flourished. But as soon as one man encroached on another man's prerogatives, the loss of balance led to disaster. The kingdom of Israel was never more extensive and more prosperous than under the reign of David, who allowed himself to be publicly lectured by Nathan and always apologized publicly for any injustices he might have committed.

In contrast, Zedekiah persecuted the prophet Jeremiah. Shortly afterwards the destruction of Jerusalem ushered in the first exile, in Babylon, in 587 BCE.

Facing page:
Gustave Doré, Samuel Blesses Saul, *illustration for the Tours Bible (1866).*

No one was better than Gustave Doré at bringing the Bible story to life. His engravings remind me of the illustrations to the biblical stories given to me as a fourth birthday present by my grandfather Abraham in Warsaw during the Occupation. How those images stirred my imagination!

Following pages:
Biagio Rebecca, Figures of the Old Testament *(eighteenth century, New College, Oxford).*

The artist Biagio Rebecca made a remarkable attempt to imagine (and "assimilate" to the Roman vision of things) the heroes of Jewish history.

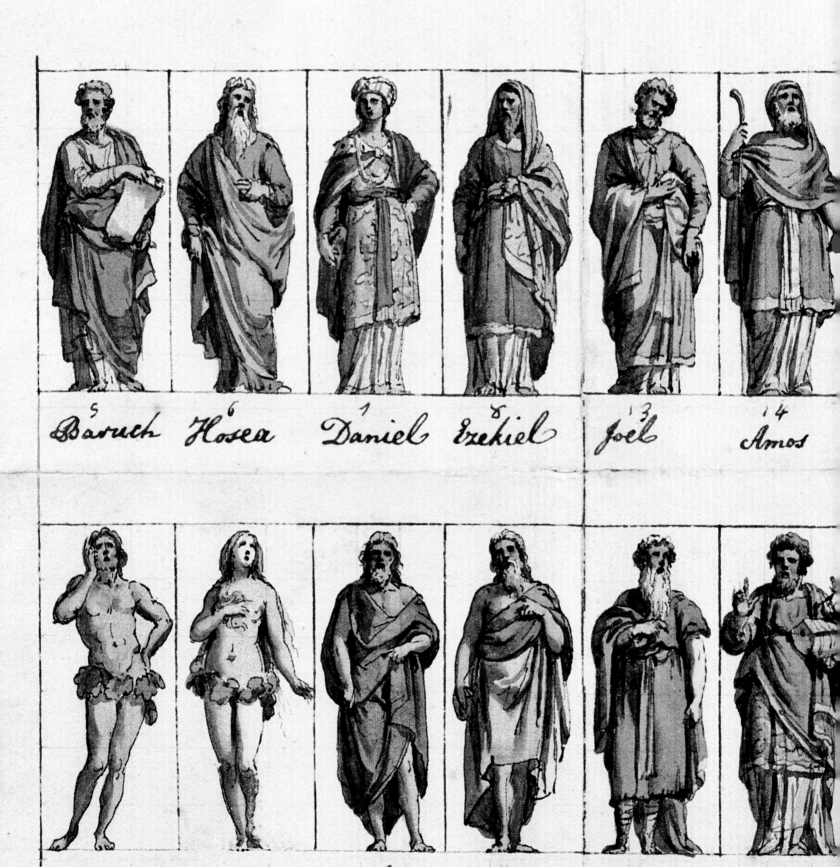

5
Baruch
6
Hosea
7
Daniel
8
Ezekiel
13
Joël
14
Amos

1
Adam
2
Eve
3
Seth
4
Enoch
9
Methusaleh
10
Noah

15 badiah   16 Jonah   21 Micah   22 Nahum   23 Habakkuk   24 Zephaniah

11 braham   12 Isaac   17 Jacob   18 Judah   19 Moses   20 Aaron

Let us follow the events step by step. If the Jewish people had three founders—Abraham, Isaac, Jacob—then the Hebrew nation was forged by three kings, three emblematic figures: Saul, David, Solomon.

The case of Saul is highly instructive. To go suddenly from the condition of shepherd to that of master of a kingdom was enough to go to anyone's head. As a king, he became melancholy, suspicious, and jealous of David, his popular—*too popular*—young servant. Saul never had time to learn the craft of kingship. David, who succeeded him, created a proper state—an empire, say some—as he pushed on to Damascus in the north and to the Red Sea in the south. He gave his people a true capital: Jerusalem, the famous Salem of Abraham's day, which he won from the Jebusites when he was thirty-seven.

David organized a professional army, appointed governors and judges, set up an administration, and levied taxes. He went down in history as a warrior king. However, since Judaism holds that a man's life cannot be limited to action, he also meditated, wrote, and communicated with the Eternal One. David was the author of much of the book of Psalms.

David's son, Solomon, although he eliminated his brother and his enemies, is remembered for his wisdom and as a man of peace. His very name, which comes from the word *shalom*, bespeaks peace. In order to pacify his borders, he invented and applied the slogan "Make love, not war"—three thousand years before 1960s California. Learning that one of his neighbors was preparing to attack, he offered to marry his daughter or sister. He lived with seven hundred wives and three hundred concubines, the master of a vast, harmonious empire.

Realizing the dream of his father David, Solomon built the Temple to house the Tabernacle with Moses' Tablets of the Law. Its style recalled the Mesopotamian ziggurats. He transformed Jerusalem, building palaces and laying out new districts. He made the city a spiritual center, one to which generations of Jews scattered across the globe would turn. Thanks to his first wife, the pharaoh's daughter, Solomon was able to develop a trade in horses—which came from

Egypt—and create cavalry forces. Thanks to his friendship with those renowned seafarers, the Phoenicians of Tyre, he developed the port of Ezion-Geber, today's Eilat. From this port on the Red Sea Hebrew boats sailed all the way to the Indies. And it was there that Solomon received the Queen of Sheba, Queen of Ethiopia. Their love would bear fruit in a son: Menelik, the first king of Africa. This extraordinary romance between the white king and the black queen has inspired hundreds of books and works of art through the centuries.

THE EMPIRE
BREAKS UP

The king's many marriages brought peace to his borders, but they also disrupted his kingdom. Solomon was tolerant and allowed his wives to keep their religions, building a temple for each one. The cost of supporting such a family soon weighed heavily on the kingdom's finances. The children fought between themselves. The court was astir with plotting. This royal expenditure was compounded by the cost of fortifying the border towns. In the king's dotage, this economic and social malaise grew so deep that it almost entirely canceled out the benefits of his great reign.

And yet the prophet Ahijah from Shiloh had warned him: because Solomon had brought idols into the kingdom, because he had not respected the exclusive covenant with the Eternal One, after his death his empire would break up. And that is what happened.

**BIRTH OF
THE TWO
KINGDOMS**

After Solomon's death, two Jewish kingdoms emerged: Judah, with Jerusalem as its capital, and Rehoboam, Solomon's son, as its king; and Israel, whose capital was Samaria and king Jeroboam. On one side, two tribes; on the other, ten. The Kingdom of Israel, also called the Kingdom of the North, kept going for two centuries, from 928 to 721 BCE. Its many kings had no great impact on the history of the Jewish people.

I shall therefore do what the Bible does, relating the history, and the stories, but selectively. I shall mention only those events that are exemplary and instructive.

**INSTRUCTIVE
STORIES**

Let us take Ahab, King of Israel. In 853 BCE he led the victors in one of the biggest chariot battles ever fought in antiquity. Confronted by 2,000 chariots and 5,542 Assyrian horsemen, the coalition headed by Ahab mustered some 3,900 chariots, 1,900 horsemen, and 1,000 camel troops. And yet, despite the scale of this battle and the thousand and one legends surely spun

Thomas Matthews Rooke, Elijah, Ahab and Jezebel in the Vineyard of Naboth *(1879, Russell-Cotes Art Gallery and Museum, Bournemouth).*

This is the story of the untrammeled power of King Ahab who, encouraged by his wife Jezebel, went so far as to kill the wine grower Naboth so he could get his hands on his vines. The prophet Elijah was there to witness and condemn the crime. The authors of the Bible rightly accorded special importance to this chapter, as if to provide a highly instructive lesson in justice.

about it by storytellers and historians, the Bible gives it barely a passing mention.

However, this same King Ahab coveted the meager vines of Naboth and had their poor farmer stoned so that he could make them his own. This action takes up a whole chapter of the Good Book. It provides a lesson. I shall follow the same principle.

DISAPPEARANCE OF ISRAEL

The kingdom of Israel lasted for some 130 years more. In 721 BCE the king of Assyria, Shalmeneser V, invaded and subjected its last king, Hoshea. Fearing that the survivors of Israel would join forces with Egypt, his successor, Sargon, led them into captivity and replaced them with peoples from the Orient. What happened to those exiles from Israel? No one knows. Their mysterious reappearances over the centuries have inspired a whole body of literature.

After the disappearance of Israel, only the kingdom of Judah intermittently perpetuated the history of the Jewish nation. Henceforth, the Hebrews would be called Judaeans or Jews.

THE HEBREWS BECOME JEWS

Don Lawrence, Samaria Falls to the Assyrians, *illustration for* The Bible Story *(1964, private collection).*

Soon one of the two Jewish kingdoms formed at the death of King Solomon would disappear. This was the end of the Israelites, as foretold by the prophet Micah in the print on p. 51, and the beginning of the history of the Jews, the sons of Judaea.

Mathieu Merian the Elder, The Religious Reforms of Josiah *(1625–27, unknown location).*

*Whenever there is difficulty—economic, political, or ideological crisis—the Jewish
People has always withdrawn into its true dwelling: language. This is what Josiah did, too.
In order to preserve the unity of a nation threatened by idolaters, he championed
the founding texts and ordered that the people read them.*

Gustave Doré, Micah Exhorting Israel to Repent,
illustration for the Tours Bible (1866).

Among the kings of Judah, two names stand out: Hezekiah and Josiah. Hezekiah built the first tunnel to supply water to Jerusalem. He ordered one team to dig from the spring of Gihon, and another to start from the city. Where the two teams met he had an inscription engraved. This is one of the oldest written documents in biblical history. However, like Josiah after him, Hezekiah owes his place in posterity mainly to the intellectuals, prophets, and artists of his reign.

The age of Hezekiah is remembered primarily for Isaiah, the "Prophet of Prophets," and Micah. The scribes of the day transcribed the prophecies of Amos, Hosea, Joel, and Jonah. The period also witnessed a key text, the Book of Job, as well as some of the psalms gathered in books III, IV, and V. Books I and II were almost entirely composed by King David. The only exception is Psalm 90, which is attributed to Moses himself.

As for Josiah, he reigned for nearly thirty-one years in the seventh century BCE. It is said that when renovating the Temple he came across a scroll of the Torah: the five Books of Moses. Upon reading these sacred texts Josiah had a revelation: he then ordered that the temples of all the pagan gods be destroyed and demanded strict observation of the ancestral laws from his subjects. Historians believe that several books of the Bible were written during this period, and that Josiah invoked these in order to cement national unity. He was one of the first Bal-Chuva, those we now call the "penitents." As such, he truly worked to restore the Law.

What role did the prophet Jeremiah play in this cultural revolution? We do not know.

The last two kings of Judah were Jehoiachin and Zedekiah. Trapped between the two great powers of the day, Babylon and Egypt, they were forced to take sides. Both ignored the advice of the prophet Jeremiah and chose Egypt. They would live to regret it. The uprising of the vassal states against Babylon, which was joined by Judah in 597 BCE, resulted in the death of King Jehoiachin and the deportation of thousands of Judaeans into Babylon. A second revolt, fomented by King Zedekiah with the help of Egypt in 588, marked the end of the kingdom of Judah. After a siege of sixteen months, the Babylonians took Jerusalem and destroyed the Temple. This happened in July and August of the year 586 BCE: the ninth day of the month of Av in the Jewish calendar.

*Herbert Gustave Schmalz,
The Daughters of Judah
in Babylon (1892,
private collection).*

*Now the Judaeans, too,
found themselves in exile.
In Babylon. With them
they took, not gold, like
the Israelites before them,
but books. Thanks to
the Text, they continued
to dream of Jerusalem
by the river of Babylon.*

Six centuries later, in 70 CE, the Roman general Titus destroyed the Second Temple, again on the ninth day of the month of Av. It would be the same for all the disasters that followed: the expulsion of the Jews from Spain in 1492, the massacres by the Cossacks in central Europe in 1648, and so forth up to the Shoah. All these tragic events took place on the ninth day of the month of Av. For the Jews, the repetition of this fateful date makes it a tragic marker in the flow of time.

The books of the Chronicles relate that, by an irony of fate, King Nebuchadnezzar of Babylon dispatched the exiles to the north of the country, between the Tigris and the Euphrates. It was from there that the tribe of Abraham had set out on its long journey southward into the land of Canaan, sixteen centuries earlier. Skilled builders and readily exploitable, many of these exiled Jews found themselves working on the huge construction sites of Babylon. While our interest in the Egyptian pyramids, built to a great extent by the work of Jewish slaves, never seems to wane, we neglect the splendor of these Babylonian edifices, built with Jewish sweat and skill. Just think of the Ishtar Gate in Berlin's Pergamonmuseum: it is forty-eight feet high, and was built by Nebuchadnezzar II in Babylon in front of the temple of the same name.

Ever since I was a child, I have felt that without the illuminating message of the Law, history is meaningless. In my memory, the memory of my parents, and of my parents' parents, from one generation to the next, we know all about the evil that takes hold of man, and about the Law set down in the Book in order to protect him from it. Is it a coincidence that the word "history"—in Greek, *historia*—should mean story, testimony?

In destroying the First Temple, Nebuchadnezzar did not put an end to the presence of Jews in the land of their ancestors, but he did usher in a new phase in the history of the Jewish people: bipolarity. On one hand, the history of the Jews in the land of Canaan, the "promised land"; on the other, the history of Jewish communities around the world—the Diaspora, or "dispersion" in Greek. By now the Jews already had a long history behind them. They had been nomadic and sedentary, slaves and then rebels, before finally becoming a free and independent people with their own land, institutions, rules, and laws. After such a long adventure, exile and dispersion changed everything.

Francesco Hayez,
The Destruction of the
Temple of Jerusalem
*(1867, Galleria d'Arte
Moderna, Venice).*

*For the Jews, after
that of the first Temple,
the destruction of
Jerusalem symbolizes
all other destruction.*

Given the mortal threat of dissolution that came with dispersion, the first, urgent priority was to preserve the profound identity of the Jewish people: knowledge, transmission, and respect for the Law. Two prophets, Jeremiah and Ezekiel, now established the framework for this new situation, the Diaspora, facing the Jews. Shortly after the first deportation, in 597 BCE, Jeremiah wrote a letter to the Judaeans, a kind of charter for Diaspora Judaism. In this text, which still reads as very modern today, he enjoined the Jews to look beyond narrow nationalism and exhorted them to integrate in foreign countries and intercede in favor of a pagan city if it was in danger.

Ezekiel, who was deported to Babylon, began to articulate a similar message in 592 BCE. When in exile, he had a vision of the Eye of God in the sky. He declared the transcendence of God: God reigns over all the earth and is present to His people, even when they are living among the nations.

The culture of the Diaspora came into being in Babylon. How were they to become integrated into a society while organizing the life of the community? And then there was the dream of return, the famous Psalm 137 (verses 1 and 5, New Jerusalem Bible):

> By the rivers of Babylon, we sat and wept at the memory
> of Zion....
> If I forget you, Jerusalem, may my right hand wither!

THE MESSIAH
OR THE DREAM
OF DELIVERANCE

The slave seeks freedom; the exile dreams of deliverance. A new idea now began to germinate within the Jewish community of Babylon, one that the Christians would make their own six centuries later: a savior of humanity would come, the Messiah. It was also in Babylon, within this same Jewish community, that the myth of the angel Gabriel first appeared, a myth taken up by Islam in the seventh century CE.

THE PERSIANS

For a little more than a generation the Jews of Babylon endured exile, living in the hope of return while faithfully observing the Law that maintained their strength and cohesion. In 539 BCE a new power rose in the East: Persia. Its king, Cyrus, conquered Babylon, Sumer, and Akkad. Judaea, too, was absorbed into his empire. Cyrus shared none of the Babylonians' historical grievances against the Jews; on the contrary, he showed real benevolence toward "the people of Moses' Law." In response to the exiles' request, he promulgated a decree authorizing the Jews of Babylon to return to Judaea:

> Cyrus, king of Persia, says this, "Yahweh, the God of Heaven, has given me all the kingdoms of the earth and has appointed me to build him a Temple in Jerusalem, in Judah. Whoever among you belongs to the full tally of his people, may his God be with him! Let him go up to Jerusalem, in Judah, and build the Temple of Yahweh, God of Israel, who is the God in Jerusalem." (Ezra 1:2–3)

Suddenly, the dream was becoming reality: and, as often happens with a desire that one never expected to become reality, the Jews of Babylon did not rush to Jerusalem. More than half a century of exile, of economic and social integration achieved thanks to the civil rights granted by the Persians, had weakened their yearning to leave. Besides, travelers returning from Jerusalem spoke of its decrepitude and of the licentiousness of the Jews there, who seemed to have turned their back on the Law.

Gustave Doré,
Cyrus Restores the Vessels of the Temple, *illustration for the Tours Bible (1866).*

Reading the story of Cyrus, King of the Persians, and his letter to the scribe Ezra enjoining him to build a Jewish kingdom in Jerusalem, one inevitably thinks of Lord Balfour, the British Foreign Minister, and the letter he wrote to Chaim Weizmann in 1917. When Cyrus II returned to the Jews the possessions of which the Babylonians had despoiled them, it was, one might say, the beginning of the "pre-Zionist" movement.

Time was passing, but the ardently desired return was no nearer. A movement we could call Zionist attempted to overcome this foolish sluggishness, to shake up the undecided and persuade as many of them as possible to take the road to their ancient homeland.

It was not until a year after the promulgation of Cyrus' decree that some 49,000 men and women, about 10 percent of the Jewish population of Babylon, set out for Jerusalem. Two men symbolized this movement homeward: Zerubbabel, the grandson of a king of Judah, and Joshua, grandson of a high priest of Jerusalem. On arriving in Jerusalem, the small group set about the difficult task of rebuilding the city and its Temple. The difficulties were legion, their resources and enthusiasm meager. The Jews who had stayed in Jerusalem during the exile had grown away from the faith and observance of the Law. How could this modest group of repatriated Jews revive the fervor of the old days?

In Judaea, relations between religion and royalty had never been easy. Old quarrels flared up again between the priests and rulers. The reconstruction of the Temple was getting nowhere.

Then Ezra entered the scene. We know very little about his life, not even where he was born. But we do know that he was a functionary of the Persian administration in Mesopotamia.

After much bargaining, Ezra received a royal order, or *firman* in Persian, described as follows:

> Artaxerxes, king of kings, to Ezra, Secretary of the Law of God of heaven: greetings!
> Now here are my orders. All members of the people of Israel in my kingdom, including their priests and Levites, who freely choose to go to Jerusalem, may go with you, for you are being sent by the king and his seven counselors to investigate how the Law of your God, in which you are expert, is being applied in Judah and Jerusalem. (Ezra 7:12–14)

Here we also learn that the exiles had preserved the full text of the Law of Moses, which was thought to have been lost centuries before. This law was now in the hands of the man whom the Persian ruler mandated to restore Jerusalem. This was in 458 BCE, two generations after the first return of the Babylonian Jews, many of whom did not stay in Jerusalem.

Gustave Doré, Cedar Are Cut Down for the Jerusalem Temple, *illustration for the Tours Bible (1866).*

Ever since King Solomon and his friendship with King Hiram of Tyre, whenever Israel needed to build or rebuild in Jerusalem, Lebanon supplied it with cedar wood.

Arriving in Judaea, Ezra sank into despair. The population had forgotten its culture and the city was threatened with ruin. But he overcame his anger and had a sudden stroke of genius: if the Jewish people had survived exile and the destruction of the Temple, he realized, without losing its identity and the strength of its faith, it was because the Temple, however prestigious, could not on its own ensure the survival of Judaism and the longevity of the Law. The Jews of Babylon were saved because they had preserved and followed the texts. By the same token, the Jews of Jerusalem had become lost because they had forgotten the texts.

Ezra therefore decided that the new Temple would be much more modest than the previous one. As for reestablishing the monarchy, that was out of the question. To replace personal power he created the Knesset Hagedolah, a Great Assembly of wise men and forerunner, two centuries before, of the Sanhedrin. To guarantee the structure of the state he introduced the study of the Law as the engine of social cohesion.

THE JEWS
BECOME THE PEOPLE
OF THE BOOK

This was the first cultural revolution in history. In order to accomplish it without violence, Ezra limited religious ceremonial to the space of the Temple, but created a second, parallel ritual that could be held anywhere and at any time: public, obligatory reading of the book of Moses by each community. Just imagine: an entire people, from Galilee to the Negev, coming out into the street at the same time and on the same day to read aloud from the same text!

Simple as it may appear, this measure changed the history of the Jews and projected them into a future that we still inhabit today. Sacrificial ceremony, that distant echo of idolatrous practices, was superseded by an awareness and respect for texts that transformed an entire people into readers and men of letters. Priests were no longer the exclusive guardians of the Law. The Jews, all together, became the People of the Book.

THE DEMOCRATIZATION
OF KNOWLEDGE

In his concern for teaching and transmission, Ezra now declared prophecy useless. This may seem surprising: why destroy this institution that allowed the faith, intelligence, and wisdom of Jeremiah, Isaiah, and Ezekiel to flourish? Ezra was a man of the future. He knew that the function of the prophets as mainstays of knowledge and champions of the people was bound to disappear now that each man could become his own prophet, fully responsible for his choices. Men no longer needed spokesmen, or to delegate their complaints. Everyone could speak in their own name. Knowledge was democratized, undermining those false prophets whose activities were still too widespread.

BEHIND EACH BOOK IS A PERSON

Ezra's reforms marked a crucial stage in the evolution of Judaism. They also manifested a biblical renaissance. Never in history had the Book acquired such importance. According to gematria, the science of assigning a numerical value to Hebrew words, the Book of the Prophets, Sefer, corresponds to the number 340. Now, if we examine all the words in the Hebrew dictionary, only one of them has this value: *shem*, or name.

Behind each book there is a name, a person. To destroy a book is to destroy a human life. That is why the Jews feel bound to preserve books, even when old and worn, moldering with damp, or crumbling from dryness. As for books that really are beyond use, a prayer is recited as they are buried, just like a human being.

The love of texts begets the love of knowledge, of memory, of thought, and of freedom. As history has constantly reminded us, when those in power attack books, it is endangering man's freedom; his very essence.

Read, say The Ethics of the Fathers: *even if you do not understand what you are reading, you will end up loving reading itself. It is this love of the Book that has enabled the Jews to survive longer than any other people, from Antiquity and through so many centuries.*

ALEXANDER THE GREAT IN JERUSALEM

I n 333 BCE, at the battle of Issus, Alexander of Macedonia routed the last Persian king of the Achaemenid dynasty, Darius III. A new era began. The Greeks took Tyre, Jerusalem, and Gaza, occupied Egypt and pressed on toward the Indies. Alexander, who, it is said, was impressed by Jerusalem and its Temple, gave the Jews complete autonomy. He guaranteed their freedom of religion and even prohibited the summoning of a Jew before the tribunal on the Sabbath. This, it would seem, was something the Greeks were often tempted to do, and the prohibition often had to be repeated.

In Alexander's time, synagogues were protected by law. The theft of the Jews' holy books was considered sacrilege and punished by confiscation of goods in favor of the public coffers. The violation of Jewish tombs was subject to harsh fines, which went to the city and the imperial tax office. Understandably then, the Jews were grateful to Alexander. In the year of his visit to Jerusalem, most newborn sons were named Alexander, and thousands of men joined his army. Jewish mercenaries were highly sought-after in ancient times.

Sebastiano Conca, Alexander the Great in the Temple of Jerusalem (1735–37, Prado, Madrid).

In his determination to make Jewish culture accessible to the Greeks, Alexander the Great introduced Hellenism into the Jewish world. The legends says that, to thank him for his friendship, the Jews offered him Solomon's library, which he in turn gave to Aristotle.

At the head of his army, Alexander marched into Asia and stopped in the borderlands of Afghanistan. His adviser and tutor, Aristotle, feared the impregnable gorges separating Central Asia and the Indies. Alexander therefore turned back. It is said that he wished to see Jerusalem once more. But Alexander fell ill during the journey and died in a village called Tikrit, (the birthplace, in modern Iraq, of Saddam Hussein). Tikrit was also where the Kurd Saladin was born, he who, centuries after Alexander, would take back Jerusalem from the Christian kings.

After his death, Alexander's generals divided up the Empire. Judaea and Egypt fell to Ptolemy I, whose dynasty treated the region very liberally throughout the third century BCE. The Jews paid taxes to the occupant but decisions were taken by a council of notables.

GREECE
IN JUDAEA

The coming of the Greeks to Judaea had a lasting influence on Judaism. It was indeed an unlikely encounter: the Jews had always looked to the East and were rooted in a Book dictated by the One God; Hellenism was based on multiple gods living in harmony with men. And yet this intellectual clash was the crucible of what would later be called Western civilization, a civilization marked by the notion of time invented by the Jews and the notion of space invented by the Greeks: on one side the Bible; on the other, Homer.

THE BIBLE
OPENS UP TO
THE WORLD

The Ptolemaic dynasty made no secret of its admiration for the Jewish people. Ptolemy II Philadelphus, who reigned over Egypt from 282 to 246 BCE, had the Torah translated into Greek. According to the legend, Ptolemy brought together seventy-two wise men, six from each of the twelve tribes of Israel, and locked them away, two to a room, on the island of Pharos, in the bay of Alexandria. Two wise men fell sick, the other seventy worked in pairs on translating the Bible. Miraculously, the thirty-five translations that resulted were all identical. This translation bears the name of Septuagint.

This first Greek translation, enriched by other Jewish texts, the originals of which were later lost, would play a central role in the advent of Christianity two centuries later. Thanks to the Greeks, the Jews discovered a world that was much vaster than they imagined, a world with which they now became passionately engaged. Jewish communities were formed throughout the Mediterranean area and flourished both intellectually and economically.

The extreme Hellenization of the Jews of Judaea met with an ultra-religious backlash, a rejection of assimilation that began with Greek culture. The Seleucid dynasty, a rival of the Ptolemies, took control of Jerusalem. One of their kings, Antiochus IV Epiphanes, "the Mad," built a pagan altar in the Temple in order to make sacrifices in honor of Olympian Zeus. Revolt followed immediately. It was led by Mattathias, a Jewish priest from the village of Modein, north of Jerusalem. Mattathias had five sons: John, Simon, Judas (known as Maccabaeus), Eleazar, and Jonathan. They were joined by thousands of pious Jews known as Hasidaeans, or *Hasidim* in Hebrew. They defeated the Greek army of Antiochus, and Judas liberated Jerusalem and its Temple.

Gustave Doré, Judas Maccabeus Pursues Timotheus, *illustration for the Tours Bible (1866).*

There is no good occupation. In the end, the Greeks turned out to be no more tolerant than the others. They wanted to force the Jews to identify with them. What followed was the great revolt of the Maccabees and the independence of Israel.

THE VICTORY
OF THE MACCABEES

In 164 BCE, on the twenty-fifth day of the month of Kislev in the Jewish calendar, three years day for day after the profanation of the Temple, the sanctuary was purified. To mark this moment Judas lit an oil lamp, the only one he could find. It should have burned for only one night, yet it lit up the Temple for eight days and eight nights. A festival "of inauguration" was instituted called *Hanukkah* in Hebrew, the "Festival of Lights."

Before his assassination in 142 BCE, Jonathan, brother of Judas, expanded the territory, restoring the old borders of Judaea. He was succeeded by his brother Simon, a prince of the Jews but also a high priest: for the first time in history, one man embodied both spiritual and temporal power. Simon minted coins and, to protect himself from enemies both to the north and to the south, declared himself, as his brother Judas had done, an ally of Rome.

INDEPENDENCE

His son John Hyrcan finally proclaimed the independence of Judaea. Thus began the Hasmonean dynasty, which marked two centuries of Jewish history. The kingdom of John Hyrcan included Transjordan, Samaria, and the Greek coastal lands. Forced conversion was common. The population of Judaea at this time is estimated at 2.5 million, 20 percent of whom belonged to Samaritan and Nabatean minorities.

Below:
Anonymous, Lighting the Menorah *(no date, private collection).*

To celebrate this victory and perhaps, even more, the miracle that followed it—the small quality of consecrated oil found in the Temple burned for eight days—every year the Jews light the Menorah for Hanukah, the festival of lights.

Following pages:
Peter Brueghel the Elder, The Census at Bethlehem *(1566, Musées Royaux des Beaux-Arts, Brussels).*

The general census imposed by Caesar Augustus meant that Joseph and his pregnant wife Mary had to travel to Bethlehem, where he was born, to have their names entered in the register kept by the Roman occupier.

The Diaspora, too, grew with extraordinary speed: 7.5 million individuals spread around the known world. According to the census ordered a century later by Augustus, the Jews represented over 10 percent of the 80 million inhabitants of the Roman Empire. It was during this census that Joseph the carpenter and the pregnant Mary of Nazareth traveled to Bethlehem.

GREATER ISRAEL

This epoch, which was also the epoch of Greater Israel, saw the formation of the political parties that have marked the life of the nation through to the present day. Two of these parties played an essential role in the time of Jesus, the Pharisees and the Sadducees. The former recruited from the middle class, the latter from the aristocracy. The Sadducees referred to the teachings of Zadok, the high priest who ministered under the reign of David; they claimed to be the sole representatives of orthodoxy, the guardians of the Torah, and rejected any attempt to interpret the texts. Conversely, the Pharisees cultivated an oral tradition and believed in the resurrection. They were popular because they opposed the rigor of the Sadducees

James Jacques Joseph Tissot, Pharisees and Herodians (Brooklyn Museum of Art, New York).

The Gospels accuse the Pharisees of all Israel's ills. But, in fact, the Pharisees were not in power: that was held by the Herodians, the administration of King Herod that governed the country for Rome, and by the Sadducees, who controlled the Temple.

and denounced corruption among the powerful, both religious and secular. In Hebrew their name is *perushim*, which means separated.

However, a minority broke away from them, accusing the Pharisees of being too lax regarding the purity of rites and the rules of both private and public life. Excluded from the party, they created communities that were like religious kibbutzim in the mountains of Judaea and on the edge of the Dead Sea. They were called the Essenes. The meaning of this name is not known, and they are mentioned neither in the Bible nor in the Gospels. It first appears in the writings of Jewish and Roman historians, such as Philo of Alexandria, Pliny the Elder, Flavius Josephus, and Tacitus. But the main reason why we know of the Essenes is because between 1947 and 1956 Bedouins discovered over six hundred of their manuscripts in eleven caves near the Dead Sea, not far from Qumran, one of their monasteries. Their doctrine and organization were similar to those of the early Christians, but these pious and nonviolent proto-Christians were not followers of Christ. They took part in the revolt against Rome. A large group of Essenes, led by a man called John, is said to have defended the northern part of Jerusalem during the siege. Many of the 960 men and woman who took their own lives in the fortress of Masada to escape the occupant were Essenes.

Several hundred Essenes rejected not only violence but also misogyny and the withdrawal of their comrades at Qumran. They took refuge at Bet Zabdai, near Damascus—hence their name, Sect of Damascus. I believe that this branch played an essential role in the advent of Christianity. It is not impossible that Mary, mother of Jesus, frequented them. This would explain why, according to the Gospels, Jesus took the road to Damascus at the end of his life, after his resurrection.

Many in the Sect of Damascus were therapists and doctors. The royal family consulted them about its illnesses. Some of them created the village of Ha Ramathaim (Arimathea) in Judaea, near today's Lod. Joseph of Arimathea, who accompanied Christ during the Passion and helped bury his body, came from there. All these figures are part of the Jewish people's odysseys.

And there is a fourth party, the Zealots. These were ultraorthodox and ultranationalist Jews. For them, the people of Israel owed obedience only to their God. They were the first to take up arms against Herod and against Rome.

Who was Herod? A vassal of Rome, certainly, but also a king of Israel who shaped the geography of the land. A great builder, it was he who expanded and embellished the Temple that the Roman emperor Titus destroyed in 70 CE, and who beautified the old town of Jerusalem. He also built many fortresses: Masada, Machaerus, Herodion south of Bethlehem, and Kypros near Jericho. He also founded Caesarea and its port.

To carry out these titanic works, he raised taxes. Already crushed by the numerous levies imposed by the Romans, the population rose up. These insurrections always started in Galilee, where the mountain terrain was well suited to guerilla warfare (the caves provided the insurgents with impregnable hiding places). Some of the resistance chiefs became famous. Among them was Judas of Gamala, known as the Galilean, and Barabbas, whose name, which recurs several times in the Gospels, means—and perhaps this is no coincidence—"son of the father" in Aramaic.

The Roman legions sent from Syria crushed these revolts one by one. The ensuing despair revived Isaiah's old prophecy: a Messiah would come. In the eyes of a sorely tried population, it seemed that only a liberator sent by the Eternal One himself would be capable of restoring hope. False messiahs, supported by false prophets, proliferated. Most of them ended up on a cross. Such was the atmosphere in which Miriam, or Mary, was born and grew up. She was the daughter of Joachim of Nazareth, a tiny village in Galilee. This makes it easier to understand why this young Jewish patriot should have dreamed of giving birth to a true liberator of Israel. And also why the chronicles of Herod's late reign are silent on the subject of this event that would have appeared to be like so many others.

The birth of Jesus, son of Miriam, Mary, and his crucifixion, which in the fourth century began to acquire the magnitude it has now, had no influence at the time on the events leading to the famous revolt against Rome and the destruction of the Temple. A century later, however, they did cause the first major schism within Judaism.

We have reached the Great Revolt of 66–70 CE and its failure. The Arch of Titus, still standing in Rome's Forum, reminds us just how important this victory was to the Romans. Defeat, too, deeply scarred the memory of the Jews, more so than the uprising of 135 CE—sixty-five years later—instigated by Bar Kokhba against the emperor Hadrian, which is said to have ended in nearly a million deaths.

If we follow the historical legend, then the failure of the insurrection in 66–70 CE and the destruction of the Second Temple by Titus were what inaugurated the scattering of the Jewish people that has continued through to present times. But the Diaspora existed well before that, in the Hellenistic age, since the reign of Alexander the Great. The Jewish communities of Babylon, Cyrenaica, Cappadocia, Alexandria, Cyprus, and Rome all felt sufficiently powerful to mount an armed confrontation with the Empire in order to force it to respect their religion and their independence. In 115–17, under the reign of Trajan, an uprising by the Diaspora ended in nearly two million deaths.

Above:
Arch of Titus, Rome, built in 81 BCE in honor of Titus's victory over the Jews in 70 BCE. Detail of relief on left interior: the triumphal procession with the seven-branch candlestick from Solomon's temple.

"Tell me who your enemy is and I'll tell you who you are." Did Rome grasp the importance of the revolt in Judaea for its image? It certainly celebrated its victory over the Jews in style.

Facing page:
Thomas Hartley Cromek, The Arch of Titus with the Colosseum (1842, private collection).

Great Rome and little Judaea. But in history, grandeur is not measured by power or population.

The year 70 CE does not mark the beginning of exile for the Jewish people, but for their God. Before then, for a period of two thousand years, the God of Israel and His People were inseparable: from Ur in Mesopotamia, the place of their first encounter, to the land of Canaan, then Egypt and the return to Canaan. In Solomon's day the Jews built for their God a dwelling that He would not leave, not even after the first destruction of Jerusalem in 597 BCE by Nebuchadnezzar, king of Babylon. Contrary to what happened in 66–70 CE, it was not God who followed the Jews but the Jews who came back to Him.

After Titus and the destruction of the Temple, this scattering of God worked to the advantage of the Christians, who built him other dwellings: in Rome, first of all, then in Byzantium. As for the Jews, they drew another lesson: if a stone and wood building could collapse under the assaults of the Romans, they must build a new indestructible one. Freud called this "the invisible edifice of Judaism."

We owe this idea to Rabbi Yohanan ben Zakkai, the spiritual leader of the revolt. With the rebel defense weakening, he negotiated with Titus to leave the besieged city and create an academy for about a hundred students at Yavneh, a small village twenty-five miles west of Jerusalem. The Roman emperor surely had no idea what his decision would lead to. The university devised by Yohanan ben Zakkai was rather unusual. As soon as a student was sufficiently knowledgeable, he took a hundred other students under his wing who, when their turn came, would each teach another hundred new students. And so on. Once again, the Jews had found a way to preserve Judaism. In a hostile world that kept them out of public life, they transmitted the knowledge and wisdom of the Law as a supreme force of resistance and action.

The "Persians, the Greeks, and the Romans have disappeared from the earth" observes Chateaubriand, who then expresses his amazement that "a little people, whose origin preceded that of the great peoples, still exists." History generally shows that when its sanctuary is destroyed and its capital is devastated, a culture will disappear. If Judaism is the exception to this rule, it is because, according to Freud, "the material edifice represented for the Jews only a visible temple, behind which lay a latent temple that was much greater, and indestructible." Chateaubriand speaks of miracles. But, without realizing it, he also offers the explanation: "Enter the homes of these people and you will find them living in dire poverty, getting their children to read a mysterious book which they in turn will give to their children. What they were doing five thousand years ago, this people is still doing today."

Sigmund Freud in his study (c. 1930).

I am not happy with Freud for Moses and Monotheism. *Did he think that by showing that the Jews played no part in the invention of monotheism he would avert Nazi wrath? He was historically wrong and failed to save the Jews anyway, and in the process defaced the very foundation of the genius of Judaism, which he so admired. This does not change the fact that he left an extraordinary body of work, and an expression that is itself enough to earn him his place in this book: "the invisible edifice of Judaism."*

Flavius Josephus Offering His Book, De Bello Judaico, *to the Emperors Titus and Vespasian, (c. 1100, Bibliothèque Nationale, Paris).*

In 75–79 CE, a long time before Chateaubriand's Génie du christianisme, Flavius Josephus wrote The Jewish War, *first in Aramaic and then in a seven-volume Greek adaptation. Along with his later book* Jewish Antiquities, *these texts form one of the most remarkable monuments to the genius of Judaism.*

FLAVIUS JOSEPHUS

I n the same period another Jew, who had also fled the fighting during the Great Revolt of 66–70 CE, had the same idea as Yohanan ben Zakkai. This was Joseph, son of Mattathias: the historian Flavius Josephus. But whereas the head of the academy of Yavneh sought to transmit the long history and travails of the Jewish people to the survivors of the disaster, Joseph sought to convey them to the nations that formed the Empire. He thus wrote this history going from ancient times to the Great Revolt of 66–70 CE in Greek. The magnificent account by Flavius Josephus provided precious information about the Jewish people's past; the initiative of Yohanan ben Zakkai safeguarded their future.

A CULTURE OF ORAL TRANSMISSION

Before the academy of Yavneh, the only Book recognized by tradition was the text composed by Moses under dictation from the Eternal One. Thus, parallel to the scrupulous transcription of the Torah by the scribes, a whole unwritten tradition had also developed. From father to son, the Jews passed down their new rules and commentaries thereon by word of mouth. These were the words that the students of Yavneh now began to compile.

EMPEROR HADRIAN INVENTS PALESTINE

In 135, as we have seen, the final revolt against Rome ended in failure. Emperor Hadrian accused the Jews of dragging him into a war he would have preferred to avoid and decided to wipe Israel off the map. He transformed even the name of Jerusalem into Aelia Capitolina, and that of Judaea into Philistia, after the Philistines, a seafaring people who came from Crete in the age of the Judges. Hence the name Palestine.

THE WRITING OF THE TALMUD

This did not put an end to the history of the Jews in their ancestral land. They would never leave it completely until the modern period. Banned from any kind of political activity, the Jews now engaged in intense intellectual activity. The academy of Yavneh moved to Usha in Galilee then, in 200, to Sepphoris. It was there, under the presidency of the scholar Yehuda Hanasi, that scribes wrote down the Mishnah, from the Hebrew for "repetition," which, influenced by the Aramaic word *Tanna,* grew to mean "study." The Mishnah brings together most of the Jewish oral laws. It would itself generate huge amounts of commentary and reflection which gave rise to a new book, the Gemara, or "complement." After Sepphoris, another academy was set up in Tiberias. It drafted the Talmud, meaning "teaching" or "study."

QVOD VATES BELLVM CREVIT NON ESSE DVELLVM
EDIDIT & MVLTIS · VOBIS QVI CERNERE VVLTIS ·
EST IOSEPHVS DICTVS FERT LIBRVM CORPORE PICTVS ·

This so-called "Jerusalem" Talmud was not the only one. Another one emerged from the Babylon Diaspora, in the academies of Sura, in the south, and Nehardea and Pumbedita in the center. The communities of Spain, Italy, France, and Germany all adopted the Babylonian Talmud.

In the first centuries of the Common Era, the fragmented edifice of the Jewish people took shape, as did the intellectual foundations of its culture. How extensive was the global Jewish population? We do not know. The Greek historian Strabo wrote, with a hint of admiration: "It would be hard to find an inhabited part of the earth that has not given refuge to this people, and where it is not master."

I had a little fun going back over the figures. The first census instituted by Augustus obliged respondents to present themselves in the head of the family's birthplace. That was why Mary, who was pregnant with Jesus, had to go to Bethlehem with Joseph. According to this census, the Jews represented 10 percent of the 80 million individuals who made up the Roman Empire. Now, as I have said, the Great Revolt of 66–70 CE caused nearly a million victims, that of 115–17 nearly two million, and, finally, that of 135 yet another million. Two centuries later, another census put the Jewish population of the empire at 6,944,000, a third of them in Palestine. If we add to this figure over a million Jewish residents in Babylon, we come back to the number recorded by Augustus in Jesus' day.

*Édouard Moyse, The
Talmud Lesson (1881,
Musée de Nancy).
Talmud: study. Sixty
treatises, commentaries
on texts and commentaries
on commentaries published,
depending on the edition,
in numerous volumes, and
written over seven centuries,
from 200 CE through to 500 BCE.*

*When a religious Jew picks
up a book, it is always the
Talmud. This is the only
holy book that is open to
the reader's knowledge: in
principle, anyone can enrich
it with their own commentary,
interpretation, or translation.
This is the case of the new
edition annotated by Rabbi
Adin Steinsalz, one of its
subtlest commentators.*

What was the cause of this population explosion? A high birth rate, for one, but also proselytism. A mosaic of peoples and religions, Ancient Rome was completely open to the existence and development of diverse communities. Thus any pagan could convert and become a full-fledged member of the Jewish people—the sons of Abraham—and share its national hope. The empire allowed freedom of association and gave each ethnic group legal status. A counsel of elders, the *gerusia*, represented the Jewish people in all its communities. Each community must possess at least one synagogue, one school, one library, ritual baths for men and for women, a canteen for the poor, a kosher butcher, a hospital, and a cemetery.

Many pagans were won over by the affirmation of a single God. The historian Flavius Josephus describes in great detail the conversion of the sovereigns of Adiabene, a small kingdom east of the Tigris integrated into the Parthian Empire.

Judaism did not encourage missionary activity. The universalism of Israel was centripetal. The purpose was not to reach out to the nations in order to convert them; rather, at the end of time, the Lord would gather the peoples to Zion. However, Judaism did have its own specific attraction: people were fascinated by its pared-down religion, its high ethical standards, and its monotheism. Furthermore, the Jews seemed to belong to a powerful brotherhood, a social and economic organization to which it was advantageous to adhere. Pagan society was in the throes of a deep crisis: the gods of the Pantheon had lost their prestige, and the Romans were looking for mystery, the hidden face of reality. Before the Christianization of the empire under Emperor Constantine (306–337), membership of the Jewish people offered both economic and spiritual advantages.

There were two stages to conversion. Before becoming a Jew, non-Jews attracted to Judaism were called "God-fearing." They stated their faith in the One God, frequented the community, followed the traditions of Israel and scrupulously adhered to the seven Laws of Noah: social justice and the prohibition of blasphemy, idolatry, incest, murder, theft, and the eating of the flesh of a living animal. The status of God-fearing did not make circumcision obligatory. The God-fearing could thus frequent Roman public baths without fear.

The proselytes, those who entered the synagogue, came mainly from the poorer classes—those for whom the bath was not a particularly important aspect of their social ascent. The term *proselyte*, "he who comes to," is taken from the Septuagint, the Greek translation of the Torah in which the Hebrew word for "stranger," *guere*, is translated no fewer than seventy times as proselyte.

Nevertheless, the word has evolved. In the first century CE it designated pagans who were prepared to become totally assimilated into the Jewish people. Philo referred to the proselyte as *epilates*, "he who comes from outside."

It was by appealing to these many God-fearing people that the early Christians were able to recruit. It was on the threshold of the synagogue that many Judeo-Christians proclaimed their difference from the Jews and their faith, the one that Jesus came to "accomplish, not abolish."

Today, we can say for sure that by proclaiming Christianity as the state religion, Constantine prevented Judaism from becoming the Roman Empire's dominant religion.

French School, The Circumcision Ceremony (eighteenth century, private collection).

Circumcision is the sign of the covenant between the Eternal One and his People. In his Voyage en Italie Michel de Montaigne, who was Jewish by his mother, Antoinette de Louppes, offers a detailed and captivating description of a circumcision in Rome.

REFORMISTS AND
REVOLUTIONARIES

Over the centuries, the Jewish people saw many reformist and revolutionary movements rise up around it, from the various forms of Christianity to the various forms of Islam. All invoked Israel, positively or negatively. All tried to convert the Jews to their new religion: in vain. The Jewish people remained the guardian of the Law that the Eternal One engraved for humanity. Even if, according to its prophets, it sometimes failed in its duty, it continued to bear witness to the divine existence.

CHRISTIANITY

First came Christianity. It was born in the very cradle of Judaism, but broke free of it. In around 62–64 CE, Saul of Tarsus, the Saint Paul of the Gospels, transformed it into a singular religion by decreeing the divine nature of Jesus. Like his successors, the Apostle Paul knew how important it was to have the sanction of Judaism.

He therefore traveled around the Jewish communities of the Mediterranean, preached in the synagogues, paid visits to influential Jews, and debated with learned men. And in keeping with Jewish law, he even circumcised Timothy, the son of a Jewess and a gentile.

But still the Jews would not follow him. They could not admit that Jesus was divine, or believe that he was the long-awaited Messiah. Saint Paul was outraged: "We had to proclaim the word of God to you first, but since you have rejected it, since you do not think yourselves worthy of eternal life, here and now we turn to the gentiles." (Acts 13:46) With the Church Fathers, this disappointment would turn to out and out hostility.

ISLAM

Almost six centuries later, another reformer, born in Mecca in 570, decided to reveal the true faith, the One God, to the polytheist nomads of the Arabian Peninsula. At the age of forty, Muhammad met the archangel Gabriel in the cave at Hira and received the first verse of the Koran.

The polytheists of Mecca, including the members of his own tribe, refused to hear of Allah. They preferred their own multiple gods, the 360 idols lined up in the Kaaba, their cubic temple. Muhammad was risking his life in Mecca: they wanted to kill him. He fled with a handful of supporters to Yathrib, later known as Medina. Such was

Turkish School,
The Archangel Gabriel Reveals the Eighth Sura to Muhammad *(c. 1595, Musée du Louvre, Paris).*

These miniatures representing Muhammad writing the suras dictated by the archangel Gabriel made me realize that, curiously enough, Judaism is the only monotheist religion that was not revealed. Only the Ten Commandments were dictated (Moses received them directly from the Eternal One); for the rest, it was men who, to my great joy, transformed their history, true or mythical, into religion.

the day of Hegira—"emigration, exile, separation"—on September 9, 622: the starting point of the Muslim calendar.

Why did Muhammad choose to flee to Medina? Because the Jews were in the majority there. Three tribes dictated their law: the Banu Qaynuqa, the Banu Nadir, and the Banu Qurayza. Convinced that the Jews would take his side against the polytheists of Mecca, Muhammad also thought that they would adopt the new form of Abrahamic monotheism that he preached: Islam, submission to a single God. "We gave the Book to the Israelites and bestowed on them wisdom and prophethood. We provided them with wholesome things and exalted them above the nations." (Koran 45:16)

The Jews gave him a friendly reception and signed a truce with him, as was customary, but did not adhere to his doctrine. Muhammad did not despair. Learning that the Jews were fasting for Ashura—the tenth day of Muharram, Yom Kippur for the Hebrews—he decided, in memory of their victory over Pharaoh, to adopt this festive day to commemorate his own victories. He also recommended that his disciples pray with their head toward Jerusalem. To win the hearts and support of the "People of the Book," he even adopted some of the Jewish rituals.

The overwhelming majority of Jews rejected his message, scandalized by the Prophet's messianic posturing. For Muhammad, the Jews consequently became a sect that "God has cursed … in their unbelief. They have no faith." (Koran 4:46). In his fury, he broke his truce with the tribes of Medina. The Banu Qaynuqa fled the city in 624, the Banu Nadir in 626, and the Banu Qurayza, who had continued to trust him, were wiped out.

PROTESTANTISM   Nine centuries later came another important reformer, Martin Luther (1483–1546). In 1542 the founder of Protestantism published a memorable anti-Semitic pamphlet: *The Jews and Their Lies*. In it he wrote: "I cannot convert the Jews. Our Lord Jesus Christ did not succeed in doing it. But I can stop up their mouths so that they will have to lie on the ground." This was his program: to burn their synagogues, confiscate their books, prohibit them from praying to God in their customary way, and force them to work with their hands or, even better, persuade the princes to expel them from their lands.

Nevertheless, in confronting both the pope and the emperor, Luther had at first hoped to gain the support and blessing of the Jews. In order to win them over, he had published a book, *Jesus Christ Was Born a Jew*, in 1523.

Our fools, the popes, bishops, sophists, and monks—the crude asses' heads—have hitherto so treated the Jews that anyone who wished to be a good Christian would almost have had to become a Jew. If I had been a Jew and had seen such dolts and blockheads govern and teach the Christian faith, I would sooner have become a hog than a Christian. They have dealt with the Jews as if they were dogs rather than human beings. The Jews are blood relatives, cousins, and brothers of our Lord. Therefore, if one is to boast of flesh and blood, the Jews are actually nearer to Christ than we are. I therefore beg our dear papists to call me a Jew when they have wearied of calling me a heretic.

Despite these words, the Jews did not rally round, and Luther took it badly.

THE COMING OF THE MESSIAH

The Jews believe in the coming of the Messiah and in the resurrection of bodies. It is from the Book of Isaiah and the tradition of Judaic monotheism that both Christianity and Islam draw their mystic faith:

"The Lord will give you a sign.... It is this: the young woman is with child and will give birth to a son whom she will call Immanuel [God is]" (Isaiah 7:14). Then: "The wolf will live with the lamb, the panther lie down with the kid, calf, lion and fat-stock beast together, with a little boy to lead them" (Isaiah 11:6). In Jewish thought, however, this vision will be realized only "after the days": at the end of history. In the meantime, the Messiah is to be found within each one of us. To find him, all mankind need only place their share of the Messiah on the table, as in an immense jigsaw puzzle: and then we would no longer need him. It is a luminous idea. Thus, for Jews, every messiah can only be a false Messiah.

At this point in my narrative, Jewish odyssey grows more complicated. Up to now, all the Jewish communities lived by the time of Jerusalem. One needed only follow events in the capital of Judaea to understand what was happening in its suburbs. But the suburbs grew into cities and the cities, countries. Each developed its own language and culture, Jewish cultures that continued to draw from the well of a Jerusalem lost and transformed into a distant hope. Hence the adage repeated at Passover: "Next year in Jerusalem."

"NEXT YEAR
IN JERUSALEM"

Next year in Jerusalem

enlightenment, destruction, renaissance

L'et's start with France. The first traces of a Jewish presence there can be found at the beginning of the Common Era, when Rome exiled Archelaus, ethnarch of Judaea, to Vienne in the southeastern department of Isère. His brother, Herod Antipas II, tetrarch of Galilee and Perea, met with an identical fate in 39 CE. He died in Lyon. No doubt they both came to Gaul with sizable retinues, forming the kernel of future communities. They certainly were not the first to settle in this country. For example, it is hard to imagine a port as influential as Marseille, which attracted much of the trade of the Orient, not having been home to Jewish merchants well before the current era.

As of 50 BCE, when Julius Caesar was distributing public lands in Sicily, Greece, the Orient, Africa, and Gaul to his legionaries, Jewish soldiers were settling in the Rhine Valley. For this we have archeological evidence. There, these men and their families learned to speak German. But in order to protect themselves from the hostility of the population, they added Hebraic words and transformed the vehicular language into their own singular language: Yiddish is the only language created out of the need not to communicate but to resist.

P. Puvis de Chavannes 1869

There were soon Jewish communities throughout France. In 629, at the request of the Byzantine emperor Heraclius, King Dagobert I expelled the Jews. They withdrew to the Mediterranean coast. In 720 the Arabs invaded Occitania from Spain. In those days Narbonne had a powerful Jewish community, and the troops of Pepin the Short laid siege to the city for a year, without success. They negotiated: if the Jews opened the city gates, Pepin would grant them the right to have their own king. And so it was that in 759 Narbonne had a Jewish monarch. He came from Babylon, was a descendant of King David, and went by the name of Natronai ben Habibai.

Charlemagne took several Jewish counselors. In 797 he asked his friend Isaac of Arles to lead an embassy to Harun ar-Rashid, the great caliph of Baghdad. Given the growing power of Byzantium and, further east, of the Khazar Empire, which had converted to Judaism, Charlemagne deemed it wise to offer a friendship and non-aggression pact to the chief of the Muslims. In the late eighth and early ninth centuries, most of the great international merchants were Jewish. They were known as Radhanites, from the Persian word for "traveler." The Persian geographer Ibn Khordadbeh observed:

> These merchant, speak Arabic, Persian, Greek, Frankish, Spanish, and Slav. They journey from West to East and from East to West, partly on land and partly by sea. They transport from the West … silks, beaver, marten, and other furs, and swords.… They embark on the Red Sea and sail from al-Kolzum to al-Jar and al-Jeddah, then they go to Sind, India, and to

14. *Levita*   13. *Sacerdote*

Squaldi dis.

Trono

Arre

Busato dis.

Stramen

15. Re

16. Soldato

'lomone

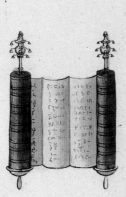

ievi

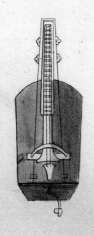

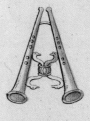

icali

Comirato inc.

China. On their return from China they carry back musk, aloes, camphor, cinnamon, and other products of the Oriental lands to al-Kolzum.... Some set sail for Constantinople to sell their goods to the Byzantines, others go to the palace of the King of the Franks to sell their wares there. Sometimes, they take the route from Rome and, passing through the land of the Slavs, come to Khamlij, the capital of the Khazars.

Toward the end of his reign, Charlemagne granted the Jews of France the right to settle their disputes in accordance with Jewish law.

RASHI IN CHAMPAGNE AND JEWISH WINEMAKERS

In the early tenth century, the center of Jewish culture in France shifted eastward, into the triangle formed by Mainz, Worms, and Troyes. This was the birthplace in 1040 of the rabbi Solomon ben Isaac, or Rashi. His academy attracted many learned men and his influence reached far beyond Champagne, where most of the winemakers were Jewish. Not one Bible was transcribed without his commentaries, or one Talmud without his explanations. To make himself easier to understand, Rashi used French expressions. A dictionary of medieval French was drawn up based on words taken from his texts.

Under the counts of Champagne, several Jewish synods were held in Troyes during the international fairs there. One of them adopted a text that gives a much clearer idea of the extent of the Jewish presence in France at the time than any partial account can do:

> That is why we, the elders and the wise men of Troyes, and those of our province, the wise men of Dijon and all around, the masters of Auxerre, of Dijon and its villages, the elders of Orléans and all around, our brothers who dwell in Chalon-sur-Saône, the wise men of the Rhine lands, our masters of Paris, the scholars of Melun and of Étampes, the inhabitants of Normandy and those of the seashore, those of Anjou and Poitiers, and the most eminent doctors of our generation, our masters of the land of Lorraine, we have taken counsel together.

It was at this time that the rabbis of Champagne revived the somewhat forgotten doctrine formulated by Rabbi Samuel in the Talmud: "The law of the land is the law." The updating of this second-century rule, which had enabled the Babylonian community to flourish, transformed relations between Jewish communities and the populations around them, allowing the Jews to become integrated into their host country while preserving their own traditions.

Above:
Anonymous, Rashi *(date and place unknown).*

Rashi, Rabbi Solomon ben Isaac, is one of the most famous commentators of the Pentateuch and the Talmud. Most of his followers were vignerons in Champagne. Whenever I'm passing through Troyes I always make sure to visit his house. I wonder, is the face in this anonymous print really a faithful likeness?

Facing page:
Eugène Beyer, The Massacre of the Jews *(1857, Musée de Strasbourg).*

Wars of religion were the most deadly wars of all. Believing themselves protected by God, men gave free rein to their death drive. Thus many Jewish communities were decimated by the Crusades.

THE JEWS IN POLAND   Starting in 1096, the First Crusade scattered the Jewish communities "to the East of Europe." Many Jews were massacred or forced to convert, while others, the majority, fled to Poland, where King Boleslaw I the Brave, who wanted men capable of developing trade and industry, encouraged them to immigrate. The Jews settled in Poland at the same time as the Khazar refugees driven out of their Jewish kingdom by the Viking tribes of Varangians and Rus.

I have always been fascinated by the Khazars. They came from eastern Turkmenistan, on the edge of Xinjiang. Driven out by the Chinese, they crossed Central Asia in the seventh century and occupied the vast territory of what is now European Russia. They built fortresses at the mouth of the Volga, near the Caspian Sea, which regional maps still call the Sea of the Khazars. They subdued the indigenous tribes and moved two friendly tribes, the Bulgars and the Magyars, towards the Danube, to guard their western borders. By the end of the seventh century they had already created a huge empire, making them the fourth global power, after only the Carolingian and Byzantine empires and the Abbasid caliphate of Baghdad. In 740 they stunned the world by converting to the Jewish religion.

This is the kingdom of the Khazars, the Turkmen tribe that converted
to Judaism in the year 740. Three centuries later, when their empire collapsed,
many of them took refuge in Poland. No doubt I too am a little bit Khazar.

We know of very few documents relating to this extraordinary adventure. What we do have are the accounts left by travelers and geographers at the time, most of them Arabs, plus a few archaeological relics, coins bearing the image of the seven-branched candelabrum, burial stones, and an astonishing correspondence in Hebrew between the rabbi Hisdai ibn Shaprut, head of the Jewish community of Cordoba, and the khan Joseph, king of the Khazars. These letters date from 960. The libraries of Christ Church College, Oxford, and Saint Petersburg both have copies. It is likely that with the fall of the Khazar Empire, in the late tenth and early eleventh centuries, some of the Khazars converted to Russian Orthodoxy, while others—a minority—withdrew into the Caucasus, where they are still known as the Mountain Jews today. The majority, however, went into exile in Poland, taking its crafts, a number of expressions that became part of the Yiddish language, and foods like *cholent* and the famous bagel—that ring-shaped bun, known as *tom* in Uighur, which started its career in Kashgar, Xinjiang, was taken by the Khazars to the bakeries of Poland, and finished its journey in the delicatessens of New York.

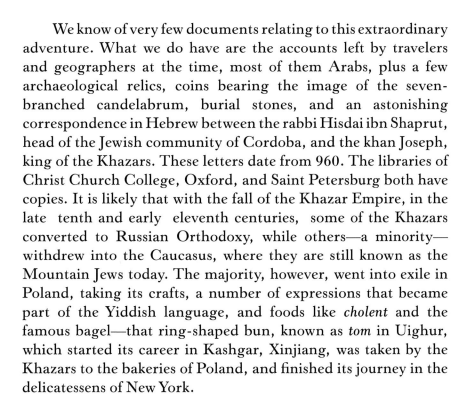

Top, left:
Window of Leon's Delicatessen, New York
(Library of Congress, Washington).

Top, right:
Kashgar, Xinjiang, China.
It is amusing to see how we today came to enjoy the bagel. First created in Kashgar, Xinjiang, it reached Poland with the Khazars and ended up in the delicatessens of New York.

Above:
Bagel seller in Warsaw in the 1920s.

Below:
*Interior of the synagogue
at Cordoba.*

*I love to explore the old
Jewish quarter, or* judería,
*of Cordoba. The decoration
of this synagogue which dates
from the caliphate period is
similar to that of a mosque.*

Facing page:
Madame Jean Tonoir, Head
of a Woman from Biskra
*(Nineteenth century, Musée
du Quai Branly, Paris).*

*We do not even have
a scrap of a portrait of
Kahina, the Jewish Berber
queen whose army twice
halted the advance of the
Islamic troops in North
Africa. And yet she must
have looked something
like this woman from
Biskra. I am sure of it.*

**THE BIRTH
OF ASHKENAZI
JUDAISM**

In the early twelfth century, then, formed by this double migratory flow of Semites from Western Europe and Turkmens from the Khazar lands, Ashkenazi Judaism came into being. Ashkenazi means "of German origin," just as Sephardic means "of Spanish origin."

**THE JEWS
IN SPAIN**

Jewish communities are thought to have settled in the Iberian Peninsula much earlier—during the biblical era, in fact. Evidence of their presence dates from the Roman Empire. When this fell, the Visigoth barbarians invaded Spain. However, they respected the rights of the Jews, who were Roman citizens at the time. Relations became much harsher in 587 when their king, Reccared I, converted to Christianity. Eight successive councils in Toledo promulgated anti-Jewish laws. A few centuries later the Inquisition would reactivate these texts that led to the expulsion of the Jews from the peninsula in 1492. This makes it easier to understand the Jews' enthusiastic response to the Muslim conquest of Spain in 711, especially since the seven thousand horsemen who defeated the Visigoths at Jerez de la Frontera were Islamized Berber Jews, descendants of the subjects of Queen Kahina.

**THE COMING
OF THE ARABS,
THE CALIPHATES**

Tariq ibn Ziyad, chief of the Berbers, gave his name to the Strait of Hercules separating Africa from Europe, Jebel Tariq, or Gibraltar. He was not a religious leader but a military one. His goal was to organize the conquered territory. For that he needed help. He tasked the Jews with setting up a new administration, developing trade, and conceiving a diplomatic structure. Mosques and synagogues were built but not very many churches, for most of the Christians had retreated to the provinces of Navarra, Leon, and Galicia. It was from there, several centuries later, that the Reconquista was launched.

In 756 the Umayyad dynasty from Syria took power in Spain, having been driven out of the Orient. Competing with its old enemy, the caliphate of Baghdad, it set out to make Cordoba the cultural center of the Arab world. Jews and Christians played an essential role. Literature and philosophy flourished, as did poetry and theater. The great library of Cordoba housed more than four hundred thousand volumes.

The better to arouse the jealousy of the Orient, the caliphs of Cordoba, Seville, and Granada set out to develop the military, economic, and cultural power of their kingdoms. The "three nations" fraternized. Under the caliphates, a rich vein of Jewish literature and philosophy developed, both in Hebrew and Arabic. The poet Judah Halevi coined the expression "the golden age of Jewish culture." He wrote books in Arabic and poems in Hebrew: love songs to the land of Israel and a book of meditations on the conversion of the Khazars.

"THE GOLDEN AGE OF JEWISH CULTURE"

In 1147 it was the turn of the Almohads from Morocco to invade Andalusia. They were sectarian—the Islamists of the day—and reproached the caliphs for their overly liberal interpretation of Koranic rules and customs, the Hadith. They burned down the library, and destroyed churches and synagogues. They transformed Andalusia into Dar al-Islam, the abode of Islam. Moses Maimonides, one of the most important Jewish philosophers, coauthor of the Arab translation of the work of Aristotle with his friend Ibn Rushd, or Averroes, was forced to convert. Many others did the same, but the Almohads mistrusted these new believers and forced them to wear a distinguishing sign: a piece of yellow cloth. Yes, even then! Only Granada allowed the Jews to prosper a little longer.

THE END OF THE ANDALUSIAN MIRACLE

Things were no better on the Christian side. As long as the kings of Castile, Ferdinand II and his successor, Ferdinand III, were fighting a national war of reconquest against the Arabs, they called themselves the "kings of the three religions." But their heirs transformed this struggle into a holy war and began to persecute the Jews and Muslims. This sectarianism engendered the theory of *pureza de sangre*, "purity of blood"—and the Inquisition. In 1492, when the fall of Granada marked the completion of the Reconquista, Isabella the Catholic expelled the Jews from Spain.

THE INQUISITION

Facing page:
Maimonides, Guide for the Perplexed *(1348, Royal Library, Copenhagen).*

It is thanks to the co-translation by the Jew Maimonides and his Arab friend Averroes that the works of Aristotle survived through the centuries.

Following pages:
Francisco José de Goya y Lucientes, The Inquisition Tribunal *(1816, Real Academia de Bellas Artes de San Fernando, Madrid).*

The Inquisition introduced the idea of "purity of blood."

SVLIMAN · OTOMAN ·
REX · TVRCX ·

der Almoral
80000 ducah

Die Cron dieses Turckischen Keisers Solimanni
ist geschätzt auf funffmal hundert tausend ducaten.

Most of them migrated to the Ottoman Empire, which welcomed them. They settled in Constantinople, Smyrna, and Salonika, and some went all the way to Jerusalem, which Suleyman the Magnificent was restoring (he built the wall that still surrounds the old center today). "You call Ferdinand a wise king," he is reported to have said, "yet in expelling the Jews he impoverished your country and enriched ours!" And so it was that many Jewish blacksmiths and powder makers enabled the sultan to increase his military potential. Jewish craftsmen, who had imported tried-and-tested techniques from Spain, quickly gained renown in the main cities of the empire. One of these Jews, Joseph Hanassi, became the chief counselor of the Sublime Porte in Constantinople and earned the title of Duke of Naxos. In reprisal for the persecution of the Jewish communities, Hanassi's aunt, Doña Gracia—a powerful woman whose story I hope to tell one day—blocked the Italian harbors on the Adriatic with her merchant fleet.

Encouraged by the Duke of Naxos, who obtained a concession for the city of Tiberias, many Spanish Jews—the Marranos, those who had been forced to convert—came to settle in Jerusalem, Zefat, Hebron, and Tiberias. Zefat developed swiftly: at the turn of the fourteenth century it had nearly ten thousand Jews, a considerable number for the time. Under the influence of the rabbi Isaac Luria, author of a highly personal interpretation of the *Zohar* and the kabbalah, Zefat became the center of Jewish mysticism.

Emanuel de Witte, Interior of the Portuguese Synagogue in Amsterdam *(c.1680, Israel Museum, Jerusalem).*

How admirable they were, these Jews who upon arriving in a new country immediately recreated their world. Witness the Portuguese synagogue in Amsterdam. Having done so, they then assimilate the country's rules and traditions. I once spent a whole night here, when the verger unwittingly locked me in. A night of much thought.

Anonymous, View of New Amsterdam
(1673, location unknown).
*New York, New York. New Amsterdam
also had its synagogues and traditions.*

The converted Jews were looking for a way to get back to the faith of their ancestors—something that Russian Jews would do centuries later. They settled in Naples, in the Netherlands, and in France in the Gironde region, in Bordeaux and in Bayonne. The mother of Michel de Montaigne, born Antoinette de Louppes, was one of them. Their great synagogue in Amsterdam, the Portuguese Synagogue, where Baruch Spinoza was excommunicated on July 27, 1656, still attracts crowds of tourists. It was among these same Jews, in the ghetto—originally the idea of a Venetian doge in 1516—that Rembrandt went looking for his subjects. Another Marrano, Rabbi Menasseh ben Israel, was one of the founders of the West India Company, which helped the Jews to settle in Brazil. In the seventeenth century they sailed along the coasts of Latin America, where the descendants of the Marranos, who had accompanied Christopher Columbus on his successive expeditions, had established prosperous communities. On September 4, 1654, they drew alongside the tip of the island of Manhattan and took part in the construction of New Amsterdam, later to become New York.

They had no idea that, three hundred years later, their small American settlement would be the biggest Jewish community in the world.

In the meantime, central Europe was where the majority of the Jewish people were concentrated. Persecuted in the West and in the Islamic countries, the Jews took refuge in Poland. The welcome they received there was so generous that the newcomers translated the name of the country, Polin, with two Hebrew words *po-lin*, meaning "here you will rest." Some Hebrew texts even named Poland Canaan in memory of the Promised Land.

Paolo Uccello, Miracle of the Desecrated Host
(c.1468, Palazzo Ducale, Urbino).

Uccello was the first painter to make dramatic use of perspective. Few artists have managed to represent the bodies of men paralyzed with fear as he has here. Their anxious gazes are fixed on the door about to break in under the blows of their persecutors. It was when I saw Uccello's The Battle *at the Louvre that I knew I wanted to be a painter.*

A great many Polish regions and villages at this time had names with a Jewish ring. Hence, as of the thirteenth century, the towns of Zydowo and Zydowska (*zyd* means Jew in Polish) near Gniezno and Kalisz. Better than any of the scant documents known to us, these names attest to the massive presence of Jews in this young kingdom.

Whenever Western Europe persecuted the Jews, the communities of Poland and Lithuania grew larger. The immigration reached a pitch in 1348, during the great plague: at Chambéry, in the Duchy of Savoy, the Jews were accused of poisoning wells. Condemned to burning at the stake, large numbers of them fled to Poland, which was still ready to welcome them.

And so, for several generations Poland attracted the Jewish populations of Italy, Bohemia-Moravia, Bavaria, Spain—a Sephardi colony settled in Lvov (today's Lviv),—and the Crimea. The unification of Poland and Lithuania considerably expanded the territory of this new kingdom, which became the second biggest country in Europe after Russia. The Jewish community of Poland grew proportionately. It now numbered over 300,000, just over 4 percent of the total population. Jewish shopkeepers and merchants became exporters, financiers, and bankers, and the lesser favored among them, farmers, craftsmen, and workers. This gave rise to a fine culture, both religious and secular.

Above:
Street of an Ashkenazim
shtetl *(1916–17).*

The shtetl was not a ghetto. It was a village inhabited solely by Jews, on the edge of the rest of society, with its own economy and language, Yiddish. This was the world of my childhood.

Facing page:
Wilhelm Arndt,
Solomon Maimon
(c.1800, BPK, Berlin).

When Christian society opened up to the Jews, the Jews joined it. Like Solomon Maimon, a disciple of Kant, they became integrated, but without losing their Jewishness.

How was it that this Jewish minority was able to acquire such important economic responsibilities within Polish society? In Poland, as elsewhere, the warrior aristocracy owned the land and held power. Its knights, the *szlachta*, waged war all over Europe and even in the Near East, wherever the good fight was to be fought. Their exploits inspired Polish literature and poetry, as was the case in France and elsewhere. But unlike his French counterpart, the king of Poland did not derive his authority from God: it was the knights, the *szlachta*, who elected him. This nobility, whom the wars often kept away from their country, rented out its monopolies— land, farms, distillation, and the alcohol trade—to the Jews, many of whom now left the cities to live in the villages, where they opened bars, the *karczma*.

The laws allowed the Jews to travel and trade freely. Often tax collectors and customs officials, they were nicknamed the "slaves of the treasury." Their immunity was such that justice punished the murder of a tax collector more severely than it did that of a knight. They enjoyed complete freedom of worship. This angered the Catholic Church, which judged their rights excessive and contrary to the "principles of the Christian faith." Out of interest or out of friendship, the nobles supported the Jews against the Church.

The Jews played an important part in the economic development of Poland. They were not the only ones: Germans, Italians, and Scots also settled in what was a thriving country. Most of these newcomers were Christians and became assimilated. The Jews kept their own faith: they became integrated, but not assimilated. Thus, in spite of the support they enjoyed, the Church managed to repress them and assign them to separate villages, neighborhoods, or streets, in order to "protect the Christian population." It was in these *shtetl* ("little towns" in Yiddish, with a Jewish majority) that they developed a solidarity which enabled them to preserve the group.

A disciple of Kant, the Jewish philosopher Salomon Maimon specified in his *Memoirs*: "There is no country besides Poland where religious freedom and religious enmity are to be met with in equal degree. The Jews enjoy there a perfectly free exercise of their religion and all other civil liberties; they even have a jurisdiction of their own. On the other hand, however, religious hatred goes so far, that the name Jew has become an abomination."

Given the hostility of the Christian populations, it is not surprising that these hundreds of thousands of men and women who spoke Yiddish, and especially the poor among them, began to dream of being together "next year in Jerusalem." This was wishful thinking, something that, in their eyes, only the Eternal One could bring about.

CHRISTIAN HOSTILITY

By a twist of history, at the end of the sixteenth century mankind discovered that Earth was much bigger than they thought, and also that it was round. They understood that the universe was infinite, sprinkled with other planets that also orbited around the sun. Because he proclaimed this loud and clear, the theologian Giordano Bruno was burned at the stake on Piazza Campo de' Fiori, Rome, on February 17, 1600. A host of astronomers got off much more lightly than he did: Nicholas Copernicus, Tycho Brahe, Johannes Kepler, and Galileo Galilei. Their discoveries and publications posed an obvious but very disturbing question: if God created other earths than Earth, then what were his plans for humankind?

And so it was that in the Renaissance the *Zohar*, the masterpiece of the kabbalah composed in Aramaic in around 1300, reappeared in Hebrew. Thanks to the invention of printing, members of the European intelligentsia, from Pico della Mirandola to Pope Clement VII and Emperor Rudolf II Habsburg, began studying Jewish and Hebrew mysticism.

As of the fifteenth century, the Jews, who were eager to share their knowledge, were among the first to embark on the adventure of printing. In 1475 they had workshops in Reggio di Calabria and Piove di Sacco, then in Ferrara and Bologna, all in Italy. In those days printers, who used engraved blocks of wood, could only print some thirty copies. The inked surface of the wood, on which the sheets of paper were placed one by one, began to disintegrate after being put through the heavy press several times.

Johannes Gensfleisch was the first person to understand that in order to print numerous copies of a text, the first thing that had to be done was to find a tougher material than wood. He is better known by the name of Gutenberg, which he took from his birthplace, a town near Mainz. Seeking refuge from his creditors in Strasbourg, which in those days was a free city, he set up his workshop on the hill of Saint-Michel, in what today is the Montagne Verte neighborhood. One day in the year 1438 he had the idea of filling letter-shaped molds with molten metal. It was a simple principle, but the problem was complex: he had to find a metal—or alloy—capable of withstanding the weight of the press. That year, helped by his associate Hans Düne and the young Jew Gabriel, son of Aaron, Gutenberg found the perfect alloy, made up of lead, iron, tin, and antimony. Extremely fluid when molten and very strong once it had set, it could be flowed into the hollow molds in order to obtain the metal characters. Once the metal had cooled, the letters could be assembled to form words and then lines.

They were inked and a sheet was placed over the ensemble. The text could then be printed on paper using the press.

The young Gabriel, son of Aaron, came from a long line of scribes. That is why, in Alsace, he was called Halter: the "guardian" of the Book. He is my direct ancestor.

THE SONCINO
BIBLE

After his revolutionary discovery Johannes Gutenberg returned to Mainz, where he printed the famous Bible that bears his name in 1454. Because he was a Jew, Gabriel, son of Aaron, known as Halter, could not obtain permission to have a printing shop in Strasbourg. In Basel, too, this was refused him. In Milan, the Jews told him about a typographer, Nathan Israel, son of the rabbi Samuel de Spire. Nathan Israel was living in Soncino, a small town in the Po Valley, not far from Cremona, later the birthplace of the famous Antonio Stradivarius. Gabriel, son of Aaron, came along at just the right moment: Nathan Israel and his two sons, Joshua Solomon and Moses, were struggling desperately to meet the orders that were flooding in for the Berakhot treatise on the Talmud with commentaries by Maimonides. The wooden letters of their press were constantly crumbling. With Gutenberg's invention, the young Gabriel had the solution to their problem. Soon, the print works at Soncino was one of the most famous Jewish presses in all Europe. It was even able to expand thanks to the patronage of Duke Francesco Sforza, who ruled over the region. The first Bible, in which the text was accompanied by the vowels, comprising 580 sheets, each having 2 columns of 30 lines, was completed in 1488. It was called the Soncino Bible.

Above, left:
Anonymous, Gutenberg and His Press in 1450 (1842, Archive of Art and History, Berlin).

Above, right:
Opening page of the Hebrew Soncino Bible, (1536, location unknown).

Ever since I found out that one of my distant ancestors, Gabriel, or "le Halter," a co-founder of the Soncino print works, worked with Hans Gensfleisch, or Gutenberg, in Strasbourg in 1435, I have thought of the inventor of mobile-type printing with admiration and tenderness.

Why, asked the Jews, does the Bible not begin with the letter *a*, the first letter of the alphabet, but instead with *b*, the second? Answer: because the first letter is God, the Creator himself; the second is His dwelling. In Hebrew, *b*, *bet*, refers to the word *bait*, "house." The Bible is thus the divine dwelling. Now, a house must be furnished, maintained, enriched, and, above all, embellished. Thus, in the Soncino Bible the letter *b* was decorated with a superb wood engraving. The first person to buy it was Pico della Mirandola. According to legend, this was the copy that Luther got hold of for his famous translation into German.

As for the house of the Jewish printers in Soncino, it still exists. It stands at the intersection of Via Lanfranco and Via della Stampa. For the five hundredth anniversary of the publication of the Soncino Bible, the Italian government decided to make La Casa degli Stampatori Ebrei a national museum: the Museo della Stampa.

The *Zohar*, a best seller of this period, is astonishing in its foresight. What the Dane Tycho Brahe and the German Johannes Kepler discovered in the observatory at Benatek, near Prague, assisted by the Jew David Ganz, the *Zohar* had described three centuries earlier:

> The earth is round like a globe [*kadur* in Hebrew] and its inhabitants differ in keeping with the climatic conditions. Because it is turning, when it is day in one half of the globe, night reigns over the other, and when light shines on one half of the earth's inhabitants, the other half is in darkness. Moreover, there are places where daylight is perpetual, where night lasts only a few moments.

If the great discoveries confirmed the descriptions in the *Zohar*, then why should this not be the case with one of its key predictions: the deliverance of the Jewish people, as foretold by the kabbalah? In this period two great messianic movements shook the Jewish communities in the Orient and in the West: that of David Reubeni in 1524 and that of Sabbatai Zevi in 1648.

David Reubeni, about whom I have written a book, landed in Venice one day on a boat that had sailed from Egypt. He was escorted by an armed guard and claimed to be the king of a distant Jewish kingdom. He did not claim to be the Messiah; rather, he saw himself as a military leader whose role it was to reconquer Israel by force of arms and to establish a Jewish state there. It was in this spirit that he proposed an alliance between Jews and Christians to Pope Clement VII. The Pope took his plans seriously and endorsed them to the king of Portugal,

Manuel I. The latter then authorized Reubeni to assemble an army of Marranos on his land. He even supplied him with arms.

A ZIONIST IDEA BEFORE ITS TIME

This Zionist plan before Zionism might have borne fruit if one of Manuel I's advisers, the young convert Diogo Pires, his mind fired by mystic writings, had not seen Reubeni as the long-awaited Messiah. Pires returned to Judaism, took the name of Solomon Molcho, and traveled round Europe and Judaea prophesying, in his homilies and books, and in quick succession, the destruction and flooding of Rome and an earthquake in Lisbon. And behold, Rome was indeed covered by the waters and Lisbon was ravaged by a fearsome quake. If Solomon Molcho had foreseen these tragedies, might he not be right in announcing the Messiah? Before ecstatic crowds, he held up David Reubeni as the emancipator of the Jewish people, thus transforming a political and military project into a messianic movement.

In those days of religious intolerance, such an undertaking was bound to fail. Solomon Molcho was burned at the stake by the Inquisition on December 13, 1532, and David Reubeni, despite the pope's friendship, disappeared into the jails of Emperor Charles V, to whom Solomon Molcho had previously proposed conversion to Judaism. This messianic movement reached as far as Prague, but not Poland.

THE ADVENTURE OF SABBATAI ZEVI

A century later, however, the movement of Sabbatai Zevi deeply shook the Jewish communities in Poland. Born in Smyrna—today's Izmir—in 1626, Zevi claimed to be the Messiah right from the start. He was twenty-two and had the support of Nathan of Gaza, a fanatical but very popular rabbi.

Zevi's messianic message seemed to offer hope to despairing communities. In 1648–49 bands of Cossacks commanded by the *hetman* Bohdan Khmelnytsky massacred the Jews of central Europe and Russia, while in Spain they faced expulsion or forced conversion, and in Morocco and Yemen persecution. After the apocalypse, said the kabbalah, deliverance would follow. Hundreds of thousands of Jews heeded the call of this new Messiah and set out for Jerusalem.

THE END OF HOPE

The Turks arrested Sabbatai Zevi in 1666. In Adrianople, today's Edirne, Sultan Mehmet IV gave him the choice between death and apostasy. Zevi chose conversion to Islam. His desertion did not prevent most of his followers from continuing to believe. But deliverance did not come.

Anonymous, Sabbatai Zevi, after the title page of the Amsterdam Tikkun *(1666, location unknown).*

The messianic dream has accompanied the Jewish people in all its peregrinations ever since the destruction of the first Temple in Jerusalem. But the demands that the Jews make of their messiah are such that nobody who lays claim to the title could prove their status. In fact, it can be said without risk of contradiction that for the Jews every messiah can only be a false messiah.

Disappointment led to disheartenment, and when the Jews are disheartened they always return to the essential: study. For that, say the rabbis, is how man can raise himself up to the level of the divine word. But for millions of Jews absorbed in their work and harrowed by fear of persecution there was no time for study. This was the root of one of the popular movements that most deeply marked Diaspora culture: Hasidism. For the Hasidim, a sincere prayer, a dance, a song, or even a cry was enough for man to be heard by the Eternal One. The *zadiks*, the just, were in charge of study, and would then share with the devout, the Hasidim, the thoughts and commentaries inspired by their readings and their frequentation of the divinity.

The founder of Hasidism was the rabbi Israel ben Eliezer, called Baal Shem Tov, the "master of the good name" in Hebrew, who was born in the Carpathians in 1700. Hasidism was organized around schools. Each had its own director and there was fierce competition between them. Some, such as the Lubavitchers, became known beyond their frontiers. They developed their own culture, complete with music, dance, and folklore. Hasidism had a deep impact on Yiddish and Hebraic literature.

This success was bound to provoke contestation. This came from the Mitnaggedim, or opponents, organized around the rabbi Elijah ben Shlomo Zalman, the Vilna Gaon—the genius of Vilna, or Vilnius. In his view, the Hasidim demagogically despised knowledge and those who possessed it so as to flatter the ignorant masses. The Pirkei Avot, or Ethics of the Fathers, were categorical: only reading and knowledge could save the world. "Read, even if you do not understand what you are reading, eventually you will love reading."

The Hasidim soon came up against a second group of adversaries: the friends of the Enlightenment, the Haskala, who were influenced by the philosophers of the eighteenth century. In Germany, where Protestantism had adopted the principle of the separation of Church and State, a number of Jews realized that they could become integrated in their adopted land without abandoning their faith. Hence the movement for emancipation which called for the recognition of civil rights for the Jews.

The German philosopher Moses Mendelssohn, a friend of Kant and grandfather of the composer, emerged as the thinker of this movement. Impressed by his work, in 1787 the French politician Mirabeau published a book on him and the struggle for Jewish rights. This inspired

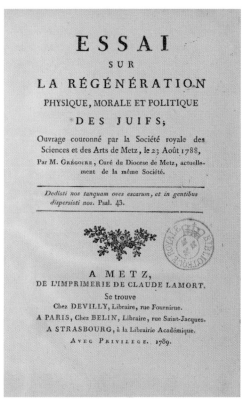

Abbé Grégoire when he came before the Constituent Assembly to champion the decrees that would grant the Jews of France civil and political emancipation.

But the Americans got there before Abbé Grégoire—or at least the State of Virginia, which included the following in its new constitution: "All men are equally entitled to the free exercise of religion, according to the dictates of conscience." At the time, this landmark decision affected only the small number of Jews living in Virginia.

LIBERTÉ des CULTES maintenue par le Gouvernement.

Un Gouvernement sage protége toutes les Religions.
Vous etes tous freres aimez tous le Gouvernement sous lequel vous vivez.

EXPLICATION

1. Buonaparte *montre l'Etre Suprême*.   3. *Juif*.   5. *Ministre Protestant*.   7. *Evêque Grec*.   9. *Mahometan*.
2. *Evêque Catolique*.   4. *Quaker*.   6. *Bonze, Prêtre Chinois*.   8. *Mesopatin*.   10. *Idolâtre des Indes*.

A Paris chez Basset Md d'Estampes et Fabriquant de Papiers peints, rue St Jacques au coin de celle des Mathurins. Nº 670.

But let us come back to the more decisive episode that was the French Revolution. When this broke out in 1789 there were four categories of Jews living in France: the Portuguese Jews of Bordeaux, Bayonne, and the surrounding areas, among whom were the converts known as the "new Christians," who installed synagogues under their churches; the Jews in the papal enclaves of the Comtat Venaissin: Avignon, Carpentras, L'Isle-sur-Sorgue, and Cavaillon; the "German Jews" of Alsace and Lorraine, who were the poorest and most numerous; and, finally, the Jews of Paris, who lived in hiding since, by virtue of the expulsion order signed on September 17, 1394, they were banned from residing in the capital and in most of the kingdom.

There are, however, many traces of a Jewish presence in Paris. In 582 Grégoire de Tours described a synagogue located exactly on the spot now occupied by the square in front of Notre-Dame. It would seem that there was also a "court of Jewry" on the land later occupied by the Bastille station and now by the opera of the same name. The whole neighborhood was Jewish at this time, and remained so until the expulsion of the French Jews by Philip Augustus in July 1182. In the Middle Ages, today's rue de la Harpe was called rue de la Juiverie. It was there, under Louis IX, that Rav Yehiel's famous yeshiva was held in 1225. In those days the Jewish cemetery extended as far as the corner now formed by the boulevards Saint-Michel and Saint-Germain. During major construction work in 1849, tombstones with Hebraic inscriptions were found there. In the thirteenth century, a time when the Talmud was being burned on the place de Grève, behind today's Hôtel de Ville, a great synagogue stood on rue de la Cité. Philip the Fair destroyed it in 1306, on the feast day of Saint Mary Magdalen. Before the Revolution there was also a Jewish caterer in rue Michel-le-Comte, another synagogue in rue des Bouchers, plus the Simon Jacob print shop in rue Montorgueil where my ancestor, Berl Halter from Alsace, worked.

The debates on the civil rights to be granted to the Jews lasted over two years. Finally, on September 27, 1791, the National Assembly passed the definitive text of the decree of emancipation. But it was the Count of Clermont-Tonnerre who clearly expressed the idea shared by most members of the Constituent Assembly: "We must refuse everything to the Jews as a nation and grant everything to the Jews as individuals."

It was Napoleon who called for the creation of a body to represent the community. The Grand Sanhédrin was founded in 1807. From now on the Jews of France had the right to manage their consistorial affairs while being considered full-fledged citizens of the Republic.

*Poster stating,
"The Government Maintains
Freedom of Worship" (1801,
Musée Carnavalet, Paris).*

*With the French Revolution,
secular messianism trumped
religious messianism.*

The effects of Jewish emancipation by the French Revolution were felt around the world. However, the Jews of Eastern Europe had to wait for the Russian Revolution of February 1917 to obtain citizen status. Not that this prevented the Bolsheviks from launching virulent campaigns against Judaism when they came to power. The Muslim lands found it harder to renounce their laws of discrimination. In North Africa the colonial powers imposed emancipation, as they did in the Levant after the First World War, in the lands of the defeated Ottoman Empire. But Yemen, for example, never abolished the discrimination that afflicted the Jews: in fact, they only obtained full civil rights by leaving the country to settle in Israel.

And the Jews of Asia? The Chinese community of Kaifeng, said to have formed under the Song Dynasty (960–1279), the communities established in the Indies in the region of Cochin from 973 BCE, lived, like other local sects, without any major problems. Likewise the Children of Israel, Bene Israel, based in and around Mumbai, who claimed to belong to the tribes of Israel deported by the king of Assyria, Tiglath-Pileser, in 722 BCE.

Below:
The Jewish Quarter of Cochin, Kerala, India.
It is enough for a Hindu to adhere to the Jewish religion for him to automatically become an heir of the Jewish tradition and to repeat, each year at Passover, "Next year in Jerusalem."

Emancipation gave the Jews of Western Europe identical rights to their fellow citizens. But it did not make the hatred suddenly disappear. The Dreyfus Affair, which broke out in 1894, is exemplary in this respect. Without emancipation, a Jew would never have been able to enter the military academy, even less the general staff of the army. One day, an act of espionage was discovered, and because Dreyfus was a Jew, he was immediately suspected of treason. Following France's National Anti-Semite League, part of public opinion became mobilized against the Jews, while other French citizens, who were initially isolated but rallied all those who defended the Republic, took the side of justice and of Dreyfus. In 1898 Zola published his famous "J'Accuse" on the front page of *L'Aurore*, the newspaper whose political editor was Georges Clemenceau.

Facing page:
Alfred de Dreux, Baron Lionel de Rothschild *(1838, NM Rothschild & Sons Ltd., London).*
It was said the Jews in the ghettos of eastern Europe had only two ways of escaping: they could become like Yehudi Menuhin or like the Rothschilds. Of course, it was easier to buy a violin than a bank, and so the violin became the great Jewish instrument. As for the Rothschilds, their status was envied but inaccessible. As my grandfather Abraham used to say: "The barouche does not cancel the anti-Semite's image of the Jews."

Intellectuals were not the only ones to defend an innocent man. Within the army, men of courage such as Georges Picquart, then head of counterespionage, also spoke out against the lies of the general staff. The Dreyfus Affair gripped and divided France for nearly ten years. It ended in 1906 with the acquittal of Dreyfus. The true guilty party, the man who had passed secret documents to the Germans, Ferdinand Walsin Esterházy, fled to Great Britain, where the Jewish community reacted violently to his arrival.

That, too, was a long story. England expelled its Jews in 1290 and they did not come back until 1656. This was under Oliver Cromwell, who negotiated their return with a rabbi in Amsterdam, Menasseh ben Israel, a friend of Rembrandt's. In 1855 David Salomons became Lord Mayor of London and, three years later, Lionel de Rothschild became Britain's first Jewish member of parliament. Another Jew, Benjamin Disraeli, twice served as prime minister to Queen Victoria, in 1867–68 and from 1874 to 1880. At the time of the Dreyfus Affair there were over three hundred thousand Jews living in Great Britain.

Deuxième Année. — Numéro 87

Cinq Centimes

JEUDI 13 JANVIER 1898

Directeur
ERNEST VAUGHAN

ABONNEMENTS

	Un an	Six mois	Trois mois
Paris	20 »	10 »	5 »
Départements et Algérie	24 »	12 »	6 »
Étranger (Union Postale)	35 »	18 »	10 »

POUR LA RÉDACTION :
S'adresser à M. A. BERTHIER
Secrétaire de la Rédaction

Adresse télégraphique : AURORE-PARIS

L'AURORE

Littéraire, Artistique, Sociale

Directeur
ERNEST VAUGHAN

LES ANNONCES SONT REÇUES :
142 — Rue Montmartre — 142
AUX BUREAUX DU JOURNAL

Les manuscrits non insérés ne sont pas rendus

ADRESSER LETTRES ET MANDATS :
à M. A. BOUIT, Administrateur

Téléphone : 102-88

J'Accuse...!

LETTRE AU PRÉSIDENT DE LA RÉPUBLIQUE

Par ÉMILE ZOLA

LETTRE A M. FÉLIX FAURE

Président de la République

Monsieur le Président,

Me permettez-vous, dans ma gratitude pour le bienveillant accueil que vous m'avez fait un jour, d'avoir le souci de votre juste gloire et de vous dire que votre étoile, si heureuse jusqu'ici, est menacée de la plus honteuse, de la plus ineffaçable des taches ?

Vous êtes sorti sain et sauf des basses calomnies, vous avez conquis les cœurs. Vous apparaissez rayonnant dans l'apothéose de cette fête patriotique que l'alliance russe a été pour la France, et vous vous préparez à présider au solennel triomphe de notre Exposition universelle, qui couronnera notre grand siècle de travail, de vérité et de liberté. Mais quelle tache de boue sur votre nom — j'allais dire sur votre règne — que cette abominable affaire Dreyfus ! Un conseil de guerre vient, par ordre, d'oser acquitter un Esterhazy, soufflet suprême à toute vérité, à toute justice. Et c'est fini, la France a sur la joue cette souillure, l'histoire écrira que c'est sous votre présidence qu'un tel crime social a pu être commis.

Puisqu'ils ont osé, j'oserai aussi, moi. La vérité, je la dirai, car j'ai promis de la dire, si la justice, régulièrement saisie, ne la faisait pas, pleine et entière. Mon devoir est de parler, je ne veux pas être complice. Mes nuits seraient hantées par le spectre de l'innocent qui expie là-bas, dans la plus affreuse des tortures, un crime qu'il n'a pas commis.

Et c'est à vous, monsieur le Président, que je la crierai, cette vérité, de toute la force de ma révolte d'honnête homme. Pour votre honneur, je suis convaincu que vous l'ignorez. Et à qui donc dénoncerai-je la tourbe malfaisante des vrais coupables, si ce n'est à vous, le premier magistrat du pays ?

⁂

La vérité d'abord sur le procès et sur la condamnation de Dreyfus.

Un homme néfaste a tout mené, a tout fait, c'est le colonel du Paty de Clam, alors simple commandant. Il est l'affaire Dreyfus tout entière, on ne la connaîtra que lorsqu'une enquête loyale aura établi nettement ses actes et ses responsabilités. Il apparaît comme l'esprit le plus fumeux, le plus compliqué, hanté d'intrigues romanesques, se complaisant aux moyens des romans-feuilletons, les papiers volés, les lettres anonymes, les rendez-vous dans les endroits déserts, les femmes mystérieuses qui colportent, de nuit, des preuves accablantes. C'est lui qui imagina de dicter le bordereau à Dreyfus ; c'est lui qui rêva de l'étudier dans une pièce entièrement revêtue de glaces ; c'est lui que le commandant Forzinetti nous représente armé d'une lanterne sourde, voulant se faire introduire près de l'accusé endormi, pour projeter sur son visage un brusque flot de lumière et surprendre ainsi son crime, dans l'émoi du réveil. Et je n'ai pas à tout dire, qu'on cherche, on trouvera. Je déclare simplement que le commandant du Paty de Clam, chargé d'instruire l'affaire Dreyfus, comme officier judiciaire, est, dans l'ordre des dates et des responsabilités, le premier coupable de l'effroyable erreur judiciaire qui a été commise.

Le bordereau était depuis quelque temps déjà entre les mains du colonel Sandherr, directeur du bureau des renseignements, mort depuis de paralysie générale. Des « fuites » avaient lieu, des papiers disparaissaient, comme il en disparaît aujourd'hui encore ; et l'auteur du bordereau était recherché, lorsqu'un *a priori* se fit peu à peu que cet auteur ne pouvait être qu'un officier de l'état-major, et un officier d'artillerie : double erreur manifeste, qui montre avec quel esprit superficiel on avait étudié ce bordereau, car un examen raisonné démontre qu'il ne pouvait s'agir que d'un officier de troupe. On cherchait donc dans la maison, on examinait les écritures, c'était comme une affaire de famille, un traître à surprendre dans les bureaux mêmes, pour l'en expulser. Et, sans que je veuille refaire ici une histoire connue en partie, le commandant du Paty de Clam entre en scène, dès qu'un premier soupçon tombe sur Dreyfus. A partir de ce moment, c'est lui qui a inventé Dreyfus, l'affaire devient son affaire, il se fait fort de confondre le traître, de l'amener à des aveux complets. Il y a bien le ministre de la guerre, le général Mercier, dont l'intelligence semble médiocre ; il y a bien le chef de l'état-major, le général de Boisdeffre, qui paraît avoir cédé à sa passion cléricale, et le sous-chef de l'état-major, le général Gonse, dont la conscience a pu s'accommoder de beaucoup de choses. Mais, au fond, il n'y a d'abord que le commandant du Paty de Clam, qui les mène tous, qui les hypnotise, car il s'occupe aussi de spiritisme, d'occultisme, il converse avec les esprits. On ne croira jamais les expériences auxquelles il a soumis le malheureux Dreyfus, les pièges dans lesquels il a voulu le faire tomber, les enquêtes folles, les imaginations monstrueuses, toute une démence torturante.

Ah ! cette première affaire, elle est un cauchemar, pour qui la connaît dans ses détails vrais ! Le commandant du Paty de Clam arrête Dreyfus, le met au secret. Il court chez madame Dreyfus, la terrorise, lui dit que, si elle parle, son mari est perdu. Pendant ce temps, le malheureux s'arrachait la chair, hurlait son innocence. Et l'instruction a été faite ainsi, comme dans une chronique du quinzième siècle, au milieu du mystère, avec une complication d'expédients farouches, tout cela basé sur une seule charge enfantine, ce bordereau imbécile, qui n'était pas seulement une trahison vulgaire, qui était aussi la plus impudente des escroqueries, car les fameux secrets livrés se trouvaient presque tous sans valeur. Si j'insiste, c'est que l'œuf est ici, d'où va sortir plus tard le vrai crime, l'épouvantable déni de justice dont la France est malade. Je voudrais faire toucher du doigt comment l'erreur judiciaire a pu être possible, comment elle est née des machinations du commandant du Paty de Clam, comment le général Mercier, les généraux de Boisdeffre et Gonse ont pu s'y laisser prendre, engager peu à peu leur responsabilité dans cette erreur, qu'ils ont cru devoir, plus tard, imposer comme la vérité sainte, une vérité qui ne se discute même pas. Au début, il n'y a donc de leur part que de l'incurie et de l'inintelligence. Tout au plus, les sent-on céder aux passions religieuses du milieu et aux préjugés de l'esprit de corps. Ils ont laissé faire la sottise

Mais voici Dreyfus devant le conseil de guerre. Le huis clos le plus absolu est exigé. Un traître aurait ouvert la frontière à l'ennemi, pour conduire l'empereur allemand jusqu'à Notre-Dame, qu'on ne prendrait pas des mesures de silence et de mystère plus étroites. La nation est frappée de stupeur, on chuchote des faits terribles, de ces trahisons monstrueuses qui indignent l'Histoire, et naturellement la nation s'incline. Il n'y a pas de châtiment assez sévère, elle applaudira à la dégradation publique, elle voudra que le coupable reste sur son rocher d'infamie, dévoré par le remords. Est-ce donc vrai, les choses indicibles, les choses dangereuses, capables de mettre l'Europe en flammes, qu'on a dû enterrer soigneusement derrière ce huis clos ? Non ! il n'y a eu, derrière, que les imaginations romanesques et démentes du commandant du Paty de Clam. Tout cela n'a été fait que pour cacher le plus saugrenu des romans-feuilletons. Et il suffit, pour s'en assurer, d'étudier attentivement l'acte d'accusation lu devant le conseil de guerre.

Ah ! le néant de cet acte d'accusation ! Qu'un homme ait pu être condamné sur cet acte, c'est un prodige d'iniquité. Je défie les honnêtes gens de le lire, sans que leur cœur bondisse d'indignation et crie leur révolte, en pensant à l'expiation démesurée, là-bas, à l'île du Diable. Dreyfus sait plusieurs langues, crime ; on n'a trouvé chez lui aucun papier compromettant, crime ; il va parfois dans son pays d'origine, crime ; il est laborieux, il a le souci de tout savoir, crime ; il ne se trouble pas, crime ; il se trouble, crime. Et les naïvetés de rédaction, les formelles assertions dans le vide ! On nous avait parlé de quatorze chefs d'accusation : nous n'en trouvons qu'une seule en fin de compte, celle du bordereau ; et nous apprenons même que les experts n'étaient pas d'accord, qu'un d'eux, M. Gobert, a été bousculé militairement, parce qu'il se permettait de ne pas conclure dans le sens désiré. On parlait aussi de vingt-trois officiers qui étaient venus accabler Dreyfus de leurs témoignages. Nous ignorons encore leurs interrogatoires, mais il est certain que tous ne l'avaient pas chargé ; et il est à remarquer, en outre, que tous appartenaient aux bureaux de la guerre. C'est un procès de famille, on est là entre soi, et il faut s'en souvenir : l'état-major a voulu le procès, l'a jugé, et il vient de le juger une seconde fois.

Donc, il ne restait que le bordereau, sur lequel les experts ne s'étaient pas entendus. On raconte que, dans la chambre du conseil, les juges allaient naturellement acquitter. Et, dès lors, comme l'on comprend l'obstination désespérée avec laquelle, pour justifier la condamnation, on affirme aujourd'hui l'existence d'une pièce secrète, accablante, la pièce qu'on ne peut montrer, qui légitime tout, devant laquelle nous devons nous incliner, le bon dieu invisible et inconnaissable. Je la nie, cette pièce, je la nie de toute ma puissance ! Une pièce ridicule, oui, peut-être la pièce où il est question de petites femmes, et où il est parlé d'un certain D... qui devient trop exigeant, quelque mari sans doute trouvant qu'on ne lui payait pas sa femme assez cher. Mais une pièce intéressant la défense nationale, qu'on ne saurait produire sans que la guerre fût déclarée demain, non, non ! C'est un mensonge ; et cela est d'autant plus odieux et cynique qu'ils mentent impunément sans qu'on puisse les en convaincre. Ils ameutent la France, ils se cachent derrière sa légitime émotion, ils ferment les bouches en troublant les cœurs, en pervertissant les esprits. Je ne connais pas de plus grand crime civique.

Voilà donc, monsieur le Président, les faits qui expliquent comment une erreur judiciaire a pu être commise ; et les preuves morales, la situation de fortune de Dreyfus, l'absence de motifs, son continuel cri d'innocence, achèvent de le montrer comme une victime des extraordinaires imaginations du commandant du Paty de Clam, du milieu clérical où il se trouvait, de la chasse aux « sales juifs », qui déshonore notre époque.

⁂

Et nous arrivons à l'affaire Esterhazy. Trois ans se sont passés, beaucoup de consciences restent troublées profondément, s'inquiètent, cherchent, finissent par se convaincre de l'innocence de Dreyfus.

Je ne ferai pas l'historique des doutes, puis de la conviction de M. Scheurer-Kestner. Mais, pendant qu'il fouillait de son côté, il se passait des faits graves à l'état-major même. Le colonel Sandherr était mort, et le lieutenant-colonel Picquart lui avait succédé comme chef du bureau des renseignements. Et c'est à ce titre, dans l'exercice de ses fonctions, que ce dernier eut un jour entre les mains une lettre-télégramme, adressée au commandant Esterhazy, par un agent d'une puissance étrangère. Son devoir strict était d'ouvrir une enquête. La certitude est qu'il n'a jamais agi en dehors de la volonté de ses supérieurs. Il soumit donc ses soupçons à ses supérieurs hiérarchiques, le général Gonse, puis le général de Boisdeffre, puis le général Billot, qui avait succédé au général Mercier comme ministre de la guerre. Le fameux dossier Picquart, dont il a été tant parlé, n'a jamais été que le dossier Billot, j'entends le dossier fait par un subordonné pour son ministre, le dossier qui doit exister encore au ministère de la guerre. Les recherches durèrent de mai à septembre 1896, et ce qu'il faut affirmer bien haut, c'est que le général Gonse était convaincu de la culpabilité d'Esterhazy, c'est que le général de Boisdeffre et le général Billot ne mettaient pas en doute que le fameux bordereau fût de l'écriture d'Esterhazy. L'enquête du lieutenant-colonel Picquart avait abouti à cette constatation certaine. Mais l'émoi était grand, car la condamnation d'Esterhazy entraînait inévitablement la revision du procès Dreyfus ; et c'était ce que l'état-major ne voulait à aucun prix.

Il dut y avoir là une minute psychologique pleine d'angoisse. Remarquez que le général Billot n'était compromis dans rien, il arrivait tout frais, il pouvait faire la vérité. Il n'osa pas, dans la terreur sans doute de l'opinion publique, certainement aussi dans la crainte de livrer tout l'état-major, le général de Boisdeffre, le général Gonse, sans compter les sous-ordres. Puis, ce ne fut là qu'une minute de combat entre sa conscience et ce qu'il croyait être l'intérêt militaire. Quand cette minute fut passée, il était déjà trop tard. Il s'était engagé, il était compromis. Et, depuis lors, sa responsabilité n'a fait que grandir, il a pris à sa charge le crime des autres, il est aussi coupable que les autres, il est plus coupable qu'eux, car il a été le maître de faire justice, et il n'a rien fait. Comprenez-vous cela ! voici un an que le général Billot, que les généraux de Boisdeffre et Gonse savent que Dreyfus est innocent, et ils ont gardé pour eux cette effroyable chose. Et ces gens-là dorment, et ils ont des femmes et des enfants qu'ils aiment !

Le colonel Picquart avait rempli son devoir d'honnête homme. Il insistait auprès de ses supérieurs, au nom de la justice. Il les suppliait même, il leur disait combien leurs délais étaient impolitiques devant le terrible orage qui s'amoncelait, qui devait éclater, lorsque la vérité serait connue. Ce fut, plus tard, le langage que M. Scheurer-Kestner tint également au général Billot, l'adjurant par patriotisme de prendre en main l'affaire, de ne pas la laisser s'aggraver, au point de devenir un désastre public. Non ! le crime était commis, l'état-major ne pouvait plus avouer son crime. Et le lieutenant-colonel Picquart fut envoyé en mission, on l'éloigna de plus loin en plus loin, jusqu'en Tunisie, où l'on voulut même un jour honorer sa bravoure, en le chargeant d'une mission qui l'aurait fait sûrement massacrer, dans les parages où le marquis de Morès a trouvé la mort. Il n'était pas en disgrâce, le général Gonse entretenait avec lui une correspondance amicale. Seulement, il est des secrets qu'il ne fait pas bon d'avoir surpris.

A Paris, la vérité marchait, irrésistible, et l'on sait de quelle façon l'orage attendu éclata. M. Mathieu Dreyfus dénonça le commandant Esterhazy comme le véritable auteur du bordereau, au moment où M. Scheurer-Kestner allait déposer, entre les mains du garde des sceaux, une demande en revision du procès. Et c'est ici que le commandant Esterhazy paraît. Des témoignages le montrent d'abord affolé, prêt au suicide ou à la fuite. Puis, tout d'un coup, il paye d'audace, il étonne Paris par la violence de son attitude. C'est que du secours lui était venu, il avait reçu une lettre anonyme l'avertissant des menées de ses ennemis, une dame mystérieuse s'était même dérangée de nuit pour lui remettre une pièce volée à l'état-major, qui devait le sauver. Et je ne puis m'empêcher de retrouver là le lieutenant-colonel du Paty de Clam, en reconnaissant les expédients de son imagination fertile. Son œuvre, la culpabilité de Dreyfus, était en péril, et il a voulu sûrement défendre son œuvre. La revision du procès, mais c'était l'écroulement du roman-feuilleton si extravagant, si tragique, dont le dénouement abominable a lieu à l'île du Diable ! C'est ce qu'il ne pouvait permettre. Dès lors, le duel va avoir lieu entre le lieutenant-colonel Picquart et le lieutenant-colonel du Paty de Clam, l'un le visage découvert, l'autre masqué. On les retrouvera prochainement tous deux devant la justice civile. Au fond, c'est toujours l'état-major qui se défend, qui ne veut pas avouer son crime, dont l'abomination grandit d'heure en heure.

On s'est demandé avec stupeur quels étaient les protecteurs du commandant Esterhazy. C'est d'abord, dans l'ombre, le lieutenant-colonel du Paty de Clam qui a tout machiné, qui a tout conduit. Sa main se trahit aux moyens saugrenus. Puis, c'est le général de Boisdeffre, c'est le général Gonse, c'est le général Billot lui-même, qui sont bien obligés de faire acquitter le commandant, puisqu'ils ne peuvent laisser reconnaître l'innocence de Dreyfus, sans que les bureaux de la guerre croulent sous le mépris public. Et le beau résultat de cette situation prodigieuse, c'est que l'honnête homme là-dedans, le lieutenant-colonel Picquart, qui seul a fait son devoir, va être la victime, celui qu'on bafouera et qu'on punira. O justice, quelle affreuse désespérance serre le cœur ! On va jusqu'à dire que c'est lui le faussaire, qu'il a fabriqué la carte-télégramme pour perdre Esterhazy. Mais, grand Dieu ! pourquoi ? dans quel but ? Donnez un motif. Est-ce que celui-là aussi est payé par les juifs ? Le joli de l'histoire est qu'il était justement antisémite. Oui ! nous assistons à ce spectacle infâme, des hommes perdus de dettes et de crimes dont on proclame l'innocence, tandis qu'on frappe l'honneur même, un homme à la vie sans tache ! Quand une société en est là, elle tombe en décomposition.

Voilà donc, monsieur le Président, l'affaire Esterhazy : un coupable qu'il s'agissait d'innocenter. Depuis bientôt deux mois, nous pouvons suivre heure par heure la belle besogne. J'abrège, car ce n'est ici, en gros, que le résumé de l'histoire dont les brûlantes pages seront un jour écrites tout au long. Et nous avons donc vu le général de Pellieux, puis le commandant Ravary, conduire une enquête scélérate d'où les coquins sortent transfigurés et les honnêtes gens salis. Puis, on a convoqué le conseil de guerre.

⁂

Comment a-t-on pu espérer qu'un conseil de guerre déferait ce qu'un conseil de guerre avait fait ?

Je ne parle même pas du choix toujours possible des juges. L'idée supérieure de discipline, qui est dans le sang de ces soldats, ne suffit-elle à infirmer leur pouvoir même d'équité ? Qui dit discipline dit obéissance. Lorsque le ministère de la guerre, le grand chef, a établi publiquement, aux acclamations de la représentation nationale, l'autorité absolue de la chose jugée, vous voulez qu'un conseil de guerre lui donne un formel démenti ? Hiérarchiquement, cela est impossible. Le général Billot a suggestionné les juges par sa déclaration, et ils ont jugé comme ils doivent aller au feu, sans raisonner. L'opinion préconçue qu'ils ont apportée sur leur siège est évidemment celle-ci : « Dreyfus a été condamné pour crime de trahison par un conseil de guerre ; il est donc coupable, et nous, conseil de guerre, nous ne pouvons le déclarer innocent ; or nous savons que reconnaître la culpabilité d'Esterhazy, ce serait proclamer l'innocence de Dreyfus. » Rien ne pouvait les faire sortir de là.

Ils ont rendu une sentence inique qui à jamais pèsera sur nos conseils de guerre, qui entachera désormais de suspicion tous leurs arrêts. Le premier conseil de guerre a pu être inintelligent, le second est forcément criminel. Son excuse, je le répète, est que le chef suprême avait parlé, déclarant la chose jugée inattaquable, sainte et supérieure aux hommes, de sorte que des inférieurs ne pouvaient dire le contraire. On nous parle de l'honneur de l'armée, on veut que nous l'aimions, que nous la respections. Ah ! certes, oui, l'armée qui se lèverait à la première menace, qui défendrait la terre française, elle est tout le peuple et nous n'avons pour elle que tendresse et respect. Mais il ne s'agit pas d'elle, dont nous voulons justement la dignité, dans notre besoin de justice. Il s'agit du sabre, le maître qu'on nous donnera demain peut-être. Et baiser dévotement la poignée du sabre, le dieu, non !

Je l'ai démontré d'autre part : l'affaire Dreyfus était l'affaire des bureaux de la guerre, un officier de l'état-major, dénoncé par ses camarades de l'état-major, condamné sous la pression des chefs de l'état-major. Encore une fois, il ne peut revenir innocent, sans que tout l'état-major soit coupable. Aussi les bureaux, par tous les moyens imaginables, par des campagnes de presse, par des communications, par des influences, n'ont-ils couvert Esterhazy que pour perdre une seconde fois Dreyfus. Ah ! quel coup de balai le gouvernement républicain devrait donner dans cette jésuitière, ainsi que les appelle le général Billot lui-même ! Où est-il, le ministère vraiment fort et d'un patriotisme sage, qui osera tout y refondre et tout y renouveler ? Que de gens je connais qui, devant une guerre possible, tremblent d'angoisse, en sachant dans quelles mains est la défense nationale ! et quel nid de basses intrigues, de commérages et de dilapidations, est devenu cet asile sacré, où se décide le sort de la patrie ! On s'épouvante devant le jour terrible que vient d'y jeter l'affaire Dreyfus, ce sacrifice humain d'un malheureux, d'un « sale juif » ! Ah ! tout ce qui s'est agité là de démence et de sottise, des imaginations folles, des pratiques de basse police, des mœurs d'inquisition et de tyrannie, le bon plaisir de quelques galonnés mettant leurs bottes sur la nation, lui rentrant dans la gorge son cri de vérité et de justice, sous le prétexte menteur et sacrilège de la raison d'Etat !

Et c'est un crime encore que de s'être appuyé sur la presse immonde, que de s'être laissé défendre par toute la fripouille de Paris, de sorte que voilà la fripouille qui triomphe insolemment.

Page 122:
Victor Lenepveu, The Traitor *(no. 6 in the* Museum of Horrors *series, 1900, The Jewish Museum, New York).*

The anti-Semitic campaign against Dreyfus is well-known Not so many know that, like Zola, a large part of the French population took the side of the Jewish captain.

Page 123:
Émile Zola, "J'accuse…!", L'Aurore (January 13, 1898, Bibliothèque Nationale, Paris).

Below:
The members of the first Zionist Congress held in Basel (Switzerland) in 1897.

The importance of the Dreyfus Affair was considerable, for Jews both in France and in other countries: it marked the beginning of political Zionism. Theodor Herzl, its creator, was the editor of a Viennese journal, the *Neue Freie Presse*. He followed the trial as its Paris correspondent. On October 27, 1894, he was deeply affected by Dreyfus's statement: "I am the victim of personal vengeance: I am being persecuted because I am a Jew." Herzl was present at the military degradation of Dreyfus. He noted: "As he passed in front of the soldiers, among whom there were many young recruits, Dreyfus frequently cried out, 'I am innocent!' Then, stopping in front of a group of journalists, he repeated: 'You must tell all France that I am innocent.'" Herzl drew two conclusions from this event. The first was that, in spite of emancipation, the Jews would never be accepted as both Jews and full-fledged citizens. Only a Jewish homeland—a Jewish homeland on the soil of Israel where they would be the majority— would ensure them full enjoyment of their rights. The second: there were, among those in power, the politicians and intellectuals, men who, out of humanism or calculation, could help the Jews obtain that state. Unlike David Reubeni, Herzl did not believe that Israel would necessarily have to be reconquered by arms.

Above:
Theodor Herzl with the first flag of Israel in the background (c.1900, anonymous photograph for a postcard).

With Herzl the religious dream of a return to Zion became a national cause.

THEODOR HERZL
AND POLITICAL ZIONISM

The first Zionist Congress was held in Basel from August 29 to 31, 1897. Theodor Herzl then traveled widely, promoting and negotiating, seeking political support for "the establishment of a national homeland for the Jewish people in Palestine."

Jewish support for Zionism was widespread and enthusiastic: the dream of "next year in Jerusalem" remained intensely alive, all the more so given the recrudescence of persecution. Only the discourse of the anti-Semites had changed: before emancipation, the Jews were condemned as "degenerates"; afterwards, they were accused of remaining just as "degenerate" *in spite of* the rights they had been granted.

Deep down, in fact, the architects of emancipation—Mirabeau and the Abbé Grégoire in France, Lessing in Germany—also thought that the Jews were degenerates. Simply, unlike Kant, Goethe, and Fichte, they refused to believe that this was inherent in their nature, which is tantamount to saying their race.

In a speech made at the Assembly during a debate on the Jews, Robespierre summed up this position inspired by Jean-Jacques Rousseau in one sentence: "The vices of the Jews are born of the abasement in which you have plunged them; they will be good when they can find some advantage in being good." As Solomon said in Ecclesiastes, there is nothing new under the sun. This idea had already been voiced by Shylock's extraordinary speech in Shakespeare's *Merchant of Venice*. "If a Jew wrong a Christian, what is his humility? Revenge. If a Christian wrong a Jew, what should his sufferance be by Christian example?" (Act III, scene 1).

Above:
John Gilbert, Shylock after the Trial.

In spite of Shylock's moving monologue in The Merchant of Venice, *the image that Shakespeare gives of the Jews in this play has always shocked me.*

Facing page, left:
The Russian Revolution of 1905.

Pogrom *is a Russian word. Ever since the massacres perpetrated in 1648–49 by Bohdan Khmelnytsky, now a Ukrainian national hero, the word has been part of Jewish reality in central Europe.*

Facing page, right:
Jewish immigrants on Ellis Island, New York (1910).

Despite the calls to solidarity and restraint by Russian intellectuals such as Leon Tolstoy, the author of War and Peace, *pogroms drove hundreds of thousands of Jews into the arms of America where, fortunately, policies regulating immigration had yet to be introduced.*

For most Jews it became obvious that laws alone were not enough to sweep away centuries of prejudice. The hope lay in changing society itself. Many joined revolutionary movements. In 1848 a great number were actively involved in the insurrections that broke out all over Europe—in Paris, Vienna, Berlin, Prague, and Rome—during the "Springtime of the Peoples." And these did indeed bring them some progress: not recognition of their specific cause, but the benefits of new social laws conceded by the threatened ruling classes.

But Jewish involvement in revolutionary movements did not overthrow anti-Jewish prejudices. On the contrary: a new stereotype, that of the subversive Jew, was added to the existing stock. Alarmed by the surge of unrest, those in power tried to deflect popular anger onto the Jews. There was a rash of pogroms. Expulsions in Moscow, massacres in Kishinev, and in Poland a general boycott of Jewish businesses.

This new wave of persecution triggered massive emigration to the United States. Between 1881 and 1914 over two million Jews crossed the Atlantic. In 1920, the United States already had 3.2 million Jews. For those who stayed in Europe, emancipation and secularization led to changes in community organization as social and educational structures replaced the old, mainly religious structures.

NEW COOPERATIVE ORGANIZATIONS

In Israel the Zionist movement set up the Office for Palestine and the first moshavs, or collective farms. In the United States, the American Jewish Joint Distribution Committee was set up in 1914 and, with the outbreak of World War I, began to put in place an international aid system. As for the Orthodox Jews, they joined together within a big political party founded in Poland, Agudat Israel (1912). The workers' movement, meanwhile, split in two: some followed the mainstream left, which organized exclusively Jewish, Yiddish-speaking sections, while others gathered in a Jewish socialist movement that aspired to social revolution while preserving their culture and language: this was the Bund, the General Union of Jewish Workers of Poland and Russia (and soon Lithuania), founded at a secret meeting held in Vilnius in October 1897.

YIDDISH

Up until World War II, the Bund played an essential role in the development of Yiddish culture and the organization of trade unions. Yiddish, the language of over ten million people, ensured the cohesion of the Jewish populations of central and Eastern Europe, and also of the American Jews, who were less religious. However, it also contributed to their marginalization within their host countries. Then again, this distinctive language gave non-Jews the impression that otherwise distinct communities formed an overall bloc with the result that, in Poland for example, politicians started learning Yiddish in order to win over Jewish voters.

Yiddish culture spawned a rich body of literature and avant-garde theater both in Eastern Europe and the United States. It irrigated the booming movie industry in America as Jewish directors fled Nazism in Europe—Josef Sternberg, Fritz Lang, Ernst Lubitsch, Otto Preminger, etc.). With them, the capital of cinema, which in the 1930s was Berlin, was transferred to Hollywood. Meanwhile, the Zionist dream was making only slow progress.

Above, top:
Fritz Lang (1963).

Above, bottom:
Ernst Lubitsch in his office in Hollywood (1935).
The Jewish artists who fled Nazi Germany played an essential role in mobilizing Hollywood, and also American public opinion, which had previously been indifferent to the rise of Hitler.

Right:
George Grosz teaching at the Arts Students League in New York (1942). From left: Josef von Sternberg, Jon Corbino, Yasuo Kuniyoshi and George Grosz.

In 1903 the Sixth Zionist Congress—Theodor Herzl's last, as he died the following year—felt the need to restate its basic principles: the settlement of Jewish farmers, workers, and tradesmen in Palestine; the organization and federation of the Jews; the consolidation of Jewish national feeling and consciousness; and the continuation of international political action in order to achieve the primary goal of Zionism, namely, the creation of a Jewish state in Palestine.

Herzl's vision was also a social one. In *The Jewish State*, the manifesto he published in 1896, he called for an eight-hour working day, unionization of the workforce, social security, the prohibition of the exploitation of local or foreign workers—equal wages for all—and the enfranchisement of women. In spite of this the Jewish Left, led by the Bund, rejected most of the Zionist program. They would, they said, make the revolution where they were living: the transformation of the Jewish condition would go hand in hand with the transformation of society as a whole.

At the time, the Jewish proletariat represented over 37 percent of the organized proletariat in Eastern Europe.

Herzl's contacts with the concerned powers in the Near East were no more encouraging. Turkey, which occupied Palestine, was opposed to the creation of a Jewish entity in a territory that it considered its own, and Germany and Great Britain withheld their support for fear of undermining their role in the region. France was less categorical. As for Pope Pius X, whom Herzl met after the Sixth Congress, he was perfectly clear: "The Jews have not recognized our Lord, therefore we cannot recognize the Jewish people."

HERZL AND
THE JEWISH STATE

PIUS X REFUSES
TO RECOGNIZE
THE JEWISH PEOPLE

A PROVISIONAL JEWISH
STATE: CYRENAICA,
UGANDA, ARGENTINA,
OR MADAGASCAR?

THE AMERICAN
COMMUNITY

Above:
Gaucho of the Argentine Republic
(1868, Library of Congress, Washington).

*The two years I spent in Argentina
make me feel close to this Jewish
gaucho—almost like family.*

Facing page:
Samuel Gompers.

*The Jews who settled in the United States
took with them a concern for social justice
and a tradition of militant unionism.
Is not solidarity the very foundation
of their community organization?*

Despairing of success, some of the delegates to the Zionist Congresses began to propose temporary homes for a Jewish state: Cyrenaica (an old Greek province in today's Libya), Mesopotamia, and then Uganda, and finally Argentina, where, with the help of a foundation created by Baron Hirsch, a few dozen thousand Jews founded settlements in the pampas: hence, soon, the "Jewish gauchos." Argentina even had its own Moiseville, or "Moses Town." Other delegates put the case for Madagascar, an idea taken up by the Nazis in their early days. But no country wanted the Jews. Did this mean that nobody would object to their disappearance?

The persecution of the Spanish and Portuguese Jews in the late fifteenth century enriched the Ottoman Empire with an influx of men and skills. In the same way, as we have just seen, the pogroms in Russia and Eastern Europe during the late nineteenth and early twentieth centuries enriched the United States of America.

Things had changed since those Marranos from Brazil founded the small Jewish community of New Amsterdam in the seventeenth century. Three centuries later, there were 3.2 million Jews in the city which became New York. Which was the stronger influence, the Jews on America or America on the Jews? The close-knit community organization that had been imposed on the first Jewish immigrants was also imported by those that followed.

When new groups of Jewish emigrants sailed to America with the Dutch East India Company in 1654, they were allowed to settle in New York only on condition that they would not become a burden on the company or on society. At the same time, their own nations were allowed to send them money. These conditions suited them: the Jewish societies of Europe and Russia were used to being mutually supportive. Then there was help from other American Jews, who felt responsible for their newly arrived brethren. Jewish immigrants brought to America their experience of social struggle. In the 1920s, three-quarters of the country's Jewish population belonged to the proletariat. They spoke Yiddish. In 1886 one of them, Samuel Gompers, founded the American Federation of Labor, which was soon a power in the land. The daily newspaper *Forward* (*Forwertz* in Yiddish) founded in 1897 by Abraham Cahan, had a print run of over 350,000. The Jewish daily press represented over 700,000 copies.

Against all expectations, in Europe, World War I and then the October Revolution strengthened Jewish aspirations to a homeland. It was true that communist Russia officially condemned anti-Semitism: on July 27, 1918, Lenin concluded a motion by the Council of People's Commissars (*Sovnarkom* in Russian), which had several Jewish members, as follows: "The Council of People's Commissars instructs all Soviet deputies to take uncompromising measures to tear the anti-Semitic movement out by the roots. Pogromists and pogrom agitators are to be placed outside the law."

It is often forgotten that Steinberg, the first commissar of justice in the young Soviet Republic, was himself a practicing Jew who would ask Lenin to suspend government deliberations when it was time for prayer. He lost his position after only six months. His comrades Trotsky, Radek, Zinoviev, and Kamenev were also Jews, but they had no wish to acknowledge the fact: they believed they were liberating the whole world. Their careers did not last much longer.

When Lenin died, in 1924, his sister Anna found out that their maternal grandfather, Alexander Dimitrievich Blank, had been

born Srul (Israel), son of Moshko Itskovich Blank, in the village of Starokonstantinov, in Volhynia province. Stalin had this hushed up, for fear of "damaging the prestige" of both Lenin and the Revolution.

Before Stalin's persecutions, the Jews enjoyed a few golden years. Yiddish was recognized as one of the national languages of the USSR and came to symbolize the break with the "nationalist bourgeoisie." The Communists used it to secularize the Jewish masses. Several newspapers in Yiddish were published in Moscow, Minsk, and Kiev, the best known being *Emes*—"The Truth," a Yiddish original version of the famous Russian *Pravda*. A Yiddish national theater, the Moscow State Jewish Theater, directed by Alexander Granovski and then by the actor Solomon Mikhoels, was set up in 1920. Marc Chagall designed sets and costumes. A Jewish publishing house brought out classic Yiddish authors such as Mendele Moykher Sforim (1836–1917), Sholem Aleichem (1859–1916), and Isaac Leib Peretz (1852–1915). Jewish painters featured in avant-garde exhibitions: Lissitzky, as well as the non-Jew Malevich, designed covers for Yiddish literary journals.

A Golden Age of Yiddish Culture

Facing page and below:
Marc Chagall, set for the Karmeny Theater in Moscow (1920, Tretyakov State Gallery, Moscow).

I marvel at the ease with which Jews manage to blend tradition and modernity, and I think with sorrow of what this Yiddish world might have produced if it had not been destroyed.

Below:
Cover of N. Shipetin's In Baheftung (volume of poems).

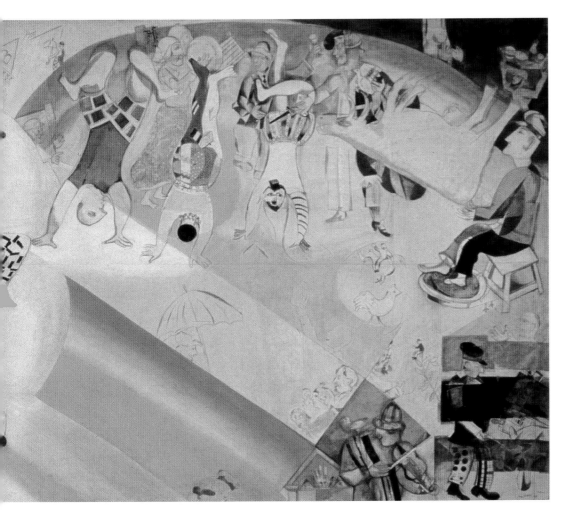

135

By making Yiddish an official language, the Communists also raised a theoretical problem. For Stalin, Lenin's successor, a nation meant a history, a language, and a territory. Now, the Jews had no territory—the Communists rejected the call for a state in Palestine, seeing it as bourgeois movement controlled by international capitalism.

BIROBIDZHAN: A RUSSIAN HOMELAND FOR THE JEWS

Another land therefore had to be found for the Jews, perhaps even in the Soviet Union itself. The Crimea was mooted. Had not the Khazars once lived there? But Stalin disliked that idea: the Crimea was too close to his native Georgia. In 1928 Kalinin, chairman of the Presidium of the Supreme Soviet, suggested an uninhabited region near the Chinese border: Birobidzhan. There were ulterior motives for this: for strategic reasons, it was very much in the USSR's interest to people this territory so as to bolster its position against the country's hereditary enemy, Japan. Stalin forced over twenty thousand Jews to head out east, accompanied, more or less voluntarily, by a few thousand Communist cadres.

In May 1934, Birobidzhan was officially declared a Jewish autonomous region (*oblast* in Russian). The inscription can still be seen today on the pediments of the railway station and on public buildings.

Birobidzhan was not the success they were hoping for. The Jews were able to express themselves in Yiddish throughout the Russian territory, and sometimes even secretly learn Hebrew, thus maintaining the hope of national renewal in the land of their ancestors. In 1939, about 40 percent of the Jewish population were living in the main cities—Moscow, Leningrad, Odessa, Kiev, Kharkov, and Dnipropetrovsk—where most of its youngsters went on to higher education.

THE GERMAN-SOVIET NONAGGRESSION PACT

In 1939–40, with the German-Soviet Nonaggression Pact, the USSR annexed the eastern part of Poland, then the Baltic States, Bessarabia, and Bukovina. This swelled the Jewish population living within Soviet borders from between two or three million to five million.

The regime's tolerance of community institutions was short-lived. They were dismantled and the Jews moved to Siberia, Kazakhstan, or, like my parents and myself, to Uzbekistan. Official anti-Semitism raised its head again and many Jewish intellectuals were shot or deported.

Propaganda poster for work on the land by the Jews of Birobidjan (1927, Musée d'Art et d'Histoire du Judaïsme, Paris).

Is this an appeal for Jews to emigrate to Israel? No, this Stalinist propaganda poster exhorts Jews to settle in Birobidjan, a faraway Siberian region of the Soviet Union.

Systemgrößen

Karoline Berg-Rolf · Leviné-Nissen · Hugo Preuss · W. Rathenau · Georg Bernhard · Isidor Weiß · Hilferding · Eissner

THE JEWS IN HITLER'S GERMANY

Hitler's rise to power in Berlin in 1933 radically changed the conditions of Jews all around the world. Germany was where the idea of emancipation had first come to the fore and, even before the Nazis took power, its society and politics had been infected by anti-Semitism. All kinds of pseudo-scientific theories emphasized the concepts of race, blood, and soil—the intellectual seedbed of Hitlerism. In fact, there were not very many Jews in Germany: 350,000 at the very most. This change was more than they could understand. One hundred thousand Jewish men had served in the army during World War I, and twelve thousand had died on the field of battle.

Jewish intellectuals had played an important role in Germany after the war. It was a Jew, Hugo Preuss, who drafted the constitution of the Weimar Republic, which became law on August 11, 1919. The dynamic Walter Rathenau, who became foreign minster in 1922, was another Jew. He was murdered by nationalist extremists on June 24 of the same year.

Above:
Karoline Berg-Rolf, Levine-Nissen, Hugo Preuss, W. Rathenau, Georg Bernhard, Isidor Weiß, Hilferding, Eissner (1934).

This rare document shows all the last defenders of democracy in Germany. All were Jews, and all were swept away by the Nazis.

Facing page:
Slogans and graffiti on the façade of a Jewish second-hand clothing store in Munich (November 9, 1938).

From the anti-Semitic tag to the coffin, there is but a short distance.

By annexing Austria in March 1938, Hitler added 190,000 Austrian Jews to those already living in Germany. After the Munich agreement of September 1938, the Reich appropriated the Sudetenland, before marching into Bohemia and Moravia and establishing a German protectorate there six months later. Thus another 400,000 Jews came under the Nazi yoke. They tried to flee but no one would take them. Some did manage to get to South and North America, while many emigrated—not without difficulty—to Palestine. Here and there in Germany, Jewish activists organized schools to prepare adults for emigration.

The Nazis encouraged and financed the anti-Semitic movements in Central and Eastern Europe. Discrimination worsened, pogroms multiplied. It was now that the idea of sending the Jews to Madagascar came up once again. But at the Evian Conference, held from July 6 to 16, 1938, in order to find a solution to the immigration of German and Austrian Jews, the only country willing to accept them was the Dominican Republic. Even the United States had begun to lower its quotas.

NO LAND OF REFUGE
FOR THE JEWS

And what of Palestine? The Jews were already creating their state before the state. Yasser Arafat often told me of his admiration for this remarkable organization that, apart from its leadership, itself a kind of government, had a parliament, an administration, a secret army, a budget, political parties, universities, trade unions, and a social welfare system. All these institutions are still in existence today. But what most astonished the world was the transformation of the country by the kibbutzim, those exemplary collective villages or socialist micro-societies.

On November 2, 1917, in the middle of World War I, the British foreign minister, Lord Balfour, published a resonant declaration to the effect that: "His Majesty's government view with favour the establishment in Palestine of a national home for the Jewish people." At last.

On January 3, 1919, in Paris, Chaim Weizmann, the future first president of the state of Israel, and King Faisal I of Iraq, to whom the British had promised a great Arab kingdom with Damascus as its capital, signed a very precise agreement concerning the establishment of diplomatic relations between the future Arab kingdom and Jewish state. Its provisions even foresaw the development of Jewish immigration, the protection of Arab farmers' rights, freedom of worship, and Muslim control of Islamic holy places. But Faisal added one condition: this accord would be valid only if Great Britain kept its promise. And Great Britain did not keep its promise, despite the help provided by the king to Colonel Lawrence in his campaign against the Ottomans and his eminent role in the capture of Damascus in October 1918. Two years earlier, in 1916, Great Britain and France had signed the Sykes-Picot Agreement, dividing up the region between themselves. The League of Nations gave France a mandate over Syria and Lebanon, while King Faisal had to content himself with a kingdom in Iraq with Baghdad as its capital.

In 1922, contrary to Balfour's promise, Winston Churchill excluded Transjordan from the Jewish national homeland, thus reducing its size by three-quarters. From now on the Jews had to fight on two fronts: against British colonial power, with its police and army, and against Arab rioters stirred up by the grand mufti of Jerusalem, Hajj Amin al-Husayni, a hater of the Jews who sided with Hitler in 1941.

In May 17, 1939, with the massacre of the European Jews already under way, Great Britain published a third White Paper further limiting Jewish immigration in Palestine. Given the increasingly alarming news from Europe, the Jews decided to call a truce with the British and 130,000 of them joined Her Majesty's Army in the fight against the Nazis. In June 1944, a Jewish brigade, advancing behind tanks flying the blue and white flag with the Star of David, took part in the liberation of Rome. The Allies also parachuted thirty-six Palestinian Jewish combatants behind the German lines so that they could attempt to save their imperiled brothers. None survived.

THE FIGHT AGAINST NAZISM

Ben Gurion declared: "We will fight the war as if there was no White Paper and fight the White Paper as if there was no war."

THE "FINAL SOLUTION"

The Nazis came to the idea of a "final solution" in stages. This can be seen from Göring's letter to Heydrich dated July 1941. It was when they understood that no one wanted their Jews—and that therefore no one would attack them for eliminating them—that they set about methodically implementing their plan to annihilate European Judaism. The first thing to do was dehumanize these Jews so that they would not revolt. They therefore dispossessed them of their names by tattooing an identifying number on their left forearm. A name has a history and history has its lessons. In spite of that, the persecuted Jews rose up in Warsaw, Bialystok, Minsk, Kaunas, and Vilnius.

Above:
The grand mufti of Jerusalem, Hajj Amin al-Husayni reviewing Bosnian Muslim volunteers recruited by the Waffen SS in January 1944.

One day, when Yasser Arafat disclaimed responsibility for what happened to the Jews of Europe, I replied that we are all responsible for what happens in the world. If he asks for my solidarity, he must show the same to me, and to my past.

THE WARSAW GHETTO UPRISING

After the war, as if in a spirit of justification, Jewish historians wrote almost exclusively about these few cases of resistance, and in particular the Warsaw Ghetto Uprising. They thus gave the impression, strange to say the least, that the sixty thousand insurgents in Warsaw in April–May 1943 somehow redeemed the honor that had been lost in cowardly fashion by the six million Jews who "let themselves" be led like lambs to the slaughter.

Facing page:
Anonymous,
The Jews Want to Fight as Jews (1944).

Do people know that during World War II nobody wanted the Jews of Palestine to fight the Nazis as Jews? In spite of English opposition, they nevertheless managed to have a brigade created in the British army.

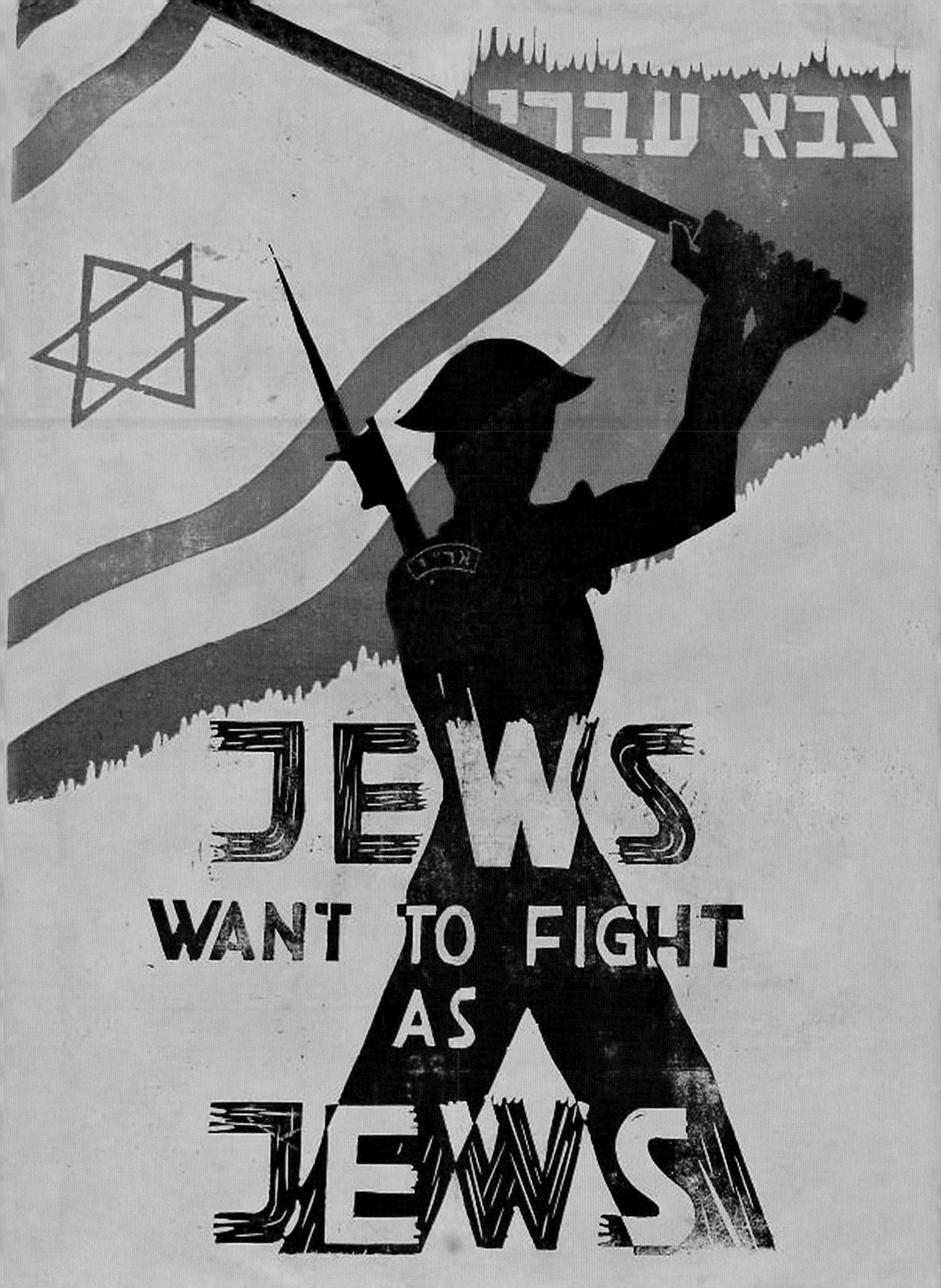
צבא עברי
JEWS
WANT TO FIGHT
AS
JEWS

Above:
Jewish religious texts found among Nazi war treasure.

n a world where violence has always been met with violence, where men celebrate the memory of Bar Kokhba, Spartacus, Joan of Arc, Giuseppe Garibaldi, and Tadeusz Kościuszko, it would seem that men only understand and appreciate armed revolt. As a result they ignore the other form of resistance that the Jews developed throughout their history. Georges Bernanos, an anti-Semite but an admirer, claimed that this resistance consisted in "withstanding and enduring." More complex and certainly less spectacular, ordained by ethics and imposed by repeated exile and dispersion, it was no less effective, for it allowed the Jews to keep going in spite of all the persecution and segregation.

When, on October 2, 1940, the Nazi governor Ludwig Fischer published the decree ordering the Jews to be transferred to the Jewish quarter of Warsaw, thereby creating the ghetto, the Jews immediately went about creating a remarkable medical, social, and cultural support network. From the very start, care was needed for the sufferings of these 500,000 men, women, and children packed into a quarter of the city initially intended for only 80,000.

The idea of the ghetto was not new, but the Nazis gave it a new magnitude. In this enclosure cut off from the rest of the world, a kind of sealed leper colony, the contagious illness was simply "being a Jew." In 1940, by its radical denial of humanity, the Warsaw Ghetto became one of the biggest ever "cemeteries of the living," a ditch where a people condemned to disappear were left to rot.

THE FIRST PHASE
OF RESISTANCE:
SPEECH

The Jews did not lose hope. They entered what I call the first phase of resistance, that of speech. Small groups of German speakers—among them my grandfather Abraham—would approach the killers and talk to them. It is almost impossible to imagine the courage and abnegation it took to engage in such a dialogue. To meet violence with words: that was their wager, their hope. One day, I have heard, my grandfather saw a Nazi catch a very young cigarette smuggler and draw his revolver to execute him. The old man held his arm and, looking him in the eye, asked, *"Warum?"* Why? Stunned, the German put the gun back in its holster and answered: *"Hier ist kein Warum"*: Here, there is no why.

I told this story to Primo Levi, who cited it in one of his books. What struck him, as it did me, is the fact that the killer had a conscience, that one could confront and talk to him. Perhaps that was why, six months later, Himmler issued a special decree forbidding German soldiers to enter the ghetto. Thus the killers would avoid until the very end the gaze and words of the condemned.

For lack of interlocutors, the Jews moved on to the second phase of their resistance: witness. In his *Notes from the Warsaw Ghetto*, the historian Emmanuel Ringelblum says that, in spite of hunger and the knowledge that they were doomed, his companions in misfortune still found the strength to gather together all the documents they could find in the ghetto. They then entrusted them to him to preserve, so that the memory would survive, and history would not erase the evils of history.

This determination to break the silence imposed on them attests to unusual daring and an intelligence that was just as rare. These men and women were acutely aware of their responsibility to future generations.

THE SECOND PHASE OF RESISTANCE: BEARING WITNESS

Coffins in a synagogue during an anti-Jewish pogrom in Lemberg, Poland (now Lviv, Ukraine), in 1918.
There are coffins for men and coffins for books. The books can be recovered. Each one, in its way, perpetuates the memory of those who are no more.

Finally, when Ringelblum and those who worked with him, who left us an irreplaceable set of documents about daily life in the Ghetto, were deported in turn, the last survivors eventually took up arms. Because there was no alternative—*ein breira*, as we say in Hebrew— the revolt opened the third and last phase of resistance, thus showing the world—since the world had its doubts—that the Jews were, like other men, capable of killing. This resistance in three phases, with the third beginning only when the first two had ceased to be effective, is for me the most intense, the most emotionally overwhelming, and the most deeply moral of lessons. The Warsaw Ghetto is above all the symbol of Jewish resistance to oppression, persecution, and death, as generations of Jews had conceived and practiced it over the centuries.

There was another form of resistance that the Jews had developed over the ages: humor.

According to Henri Bergson (*Laughter*, 1900), man is "an animal which laughs." Bergson adds that we find it difficult—unless, that is, we stifle our emotions—to laugh at someone who makes us feel pity.

And so, in order to avoid both pity and hatred, the Jews invented another category of laughter: laughter at oneself. This was a way of preempting and disarming the irony, sarcasm, and caricatures directed at them. This laughter, which is known as "Jewish humor," plays on the displacement of words and situations. For example, on hearing of the first roundups of French Jews, the playwright Tristan Bernard said: "I belong to the elect ... well, they're holding the second ballot right now." And, on arriving at the Drancy camp, the antechamber to Auschwitz: "Up to now we were living in dread, from now on we shall live in hope."

The writer Piotr Rawicz, who escaped from Auschwitz, was very sensitive to cold. Even in the summer, he wore a cardigan. People were constantly asking him why: he replied that ever since he had come out of the ovens he was always feeling cold.

In his book *Jokes and Their Relation to the Unconscious* (1905), Freud liberally peppered his argument with Jewish jokes. He justified his method thus: "we do not insist upon a patent of nobility from our examples. We make no inquiries about their origin but only about their efficiency—whether they are capable of making us laugh and whether they deserve our theoretical interest. And both these two requirements are best fulfilled precisely by Jewish jokes."

Freud quotes one of the witticisms that made him laugh, one that neatly describes the Jewish condition: "Never to be born would be the best thing for mortal men. ... But this happens to scarcely one person in a hundred thousand." Many other jokes illustrate this self-mocking tone characteristic of Jewish humor. For example, the Jew in a travel agent's office trying to choose the country he will emigrate to. The employee shows him a globe and describes the dangers of each destination: here the Jews are refused entry, there the whole population lives in poverty, elsewhere the Jews are persecuted, and so on. The Jew is uncomfortable and looks sadly at the globe, then asks: "Don't you have any others?" Another joke: passing through a town that has a large Jewish community, Khrushchev asks to meet the rabbi. "There isn't one," the official replies. "The rabbi has died and we were unable to replace him." "Why?" asks Khrushchev. "Well, there were three candidates to succeed the rabbi but none of them was suitable. The first had a rabbi's diploma but wasn't a member of the Party. The second was a member of the Party but didn't have the diploma. The third had the diploma and was a member of the Party, but there was a problem: he was a Jew."

From Job to Marc Bloch, the message is the same: memory helps us to choose, it brings the benefit of experience and grounds History in the Law. What does Deuteronomy say? "I am offering you life or death, blessing or curse. Choose life."

One cannot evoke Judaism by evoking only evil and its efforts to protect itself from it. That would be to forget justice, which was of such concern to Moses. Can good exist without justice? According to the Talmud, a minimum of thirty-six righteous men are needed to sustain the world. According to the *gematria*, thirty-six represents two times eighteen, that is to say, two times life, for the number eighteen corresponds to the word *hai*, "life" or, better, "life that saves life."

It was in Poland that there was the greatest number of righteous men, that is to say, non-Jews who risked their lives to hide Jews under the German occupation. That is logical: Poland had the greatest number of Jews. But it was in France that the righteous men saved the greatest number of lives. Out of the 300,000 Jews living in France before the war, over two-thirds survived thanks to simple men and women who considered it their duty to help those who were persecuted. They did so despite the active collaboration of the French police and militia with the German SS in both Vichy and Occupied France.

VASUL „STRUMA" TRANSPORT DE EMIGRANȚI EVREI ÎN PALESTINA
Plecarea: 8 Octombrie 1941 din Constanța
LOCURI LIMITATE
Informațiuni și înscrieri la: Comitetul „ALYIA"
de pe lângă noua organizație Sionistă, Calea Moșilor 78, Etaj 1, și
Biroul de Voiaj „TURISMUL MONDIAL" Calea Victoriei 100

David Stoliar, now a rich business-man (far left), first heard of the existence of the Struma through the advertisement (above) in a Romanian newspaper. It seemed that the only problem in getting to Palestine was the limited num-ber of places left. Stoliar bought a ticket (left). The Struma, grossly overcrowded, crawled into Istanbul. The British, unwilling to risk Arab hostility to further Jewish immigration at this crucial time, refused to clear the boat for Palestine. She was towed out of Turkish waters and was sunk, probably by torpedo, on Febru-ary 24, 1942 (below). Jewish terror-ists accused the British High Commissioner of murder (far left)

709 REFUGEES LOST IN STRUMA; SHIP SINKS IN BLACK SEA
Agency Statement on Efforts to Save Fugitives

It was learned officially in Jerusalem yesterday from the British Embassy in An-kara that, according to the semi-official Anadolu news

Left:
Identity card of David Stoliar (United States Holocaust Memorial Museum, Washington).

Quite a shock, this ID card of the only survivor from the 709 refugees packed into that old tub called the Struma. It was February 1942. They were all Jews and nobody wanted them. Doesn't this story remind us of all those boat people who still sail over the oceans and seas today?

Facing page:
"Never has a Hollywood film done so much good": that is what David Ben Gurion liked to say of Otto Preminger's Exodus, *which relates the odyssey of the eponymous boat filled with survivors from the death camps who dreamed of reaching the coast of Israel.*

At this stage of my story, I cannot hold back this burning question, one that will always exercise me: why didn't the others, all the others, take the same salutary action? What *were* the English and the Turks thinking of when they refused passage to the *Struma*, the ship packed with Romanian Jews fleeing death? After three months of uncertainty, the boat was towed out into the Black Sea by the Turkish navy. There it sank on February 24, 1942, having been torpedoed by a Soviet submarine. Out of seven hundred and seventy passengers, only one survived: David Stoleru. Exhausted by their Herculean task of liquidating six million human beings, the German killers were prepared to let a number of them go. It is said that seventy thousand people had, in exchange for a ransom, been given permission to take refuge in France. But, as with the price for saving the Hungarian Jews—a million women, men, and children in exchange for trucks and strategic material—the Allies refused. This was in 1944.

Not long ago, a Catholic priest, Father Patrick Desbois, went out to Ukraine, where his grandfather was deported. It is thanks to him that we now know that, even before the "Final Solution" was put in place by the Germans, local populations had already liquidated some of their Jews. Father Desbois called this massacre the "Holocaust by bullets." In this light it is easier to understand the joy of the survivors, many of them anti-Zionists, at the proclamation of the State of Israel.

THE "HOLOCAUST BY BULLETS"

As Israel's first president, Chaim Weizmann, said: "No state is given to its people on a silver platter." Of course, this fledgling nation in Palestine did benefit from the universal guilty conscience: the Jews had been abandoned, left to Hitler. And, in spite of the revelations about the camps and the ovens, the English still stopped the dilapidated boats packed with Jewish survivors heading for Israel—or, even worse, scuttled them. All this took place amid international indifference. World opinion only really woke up when the *Exodus*, an American ship carrying 4,500 Jews, which set sail from Sète in France, endured all kinds of obstacles and betrayed hopes only to be taken back to Hamburg and the land of the killers.

THE EXODUS

Exodus (1947).

Exodus, Exodus... *I should have been on this ship with my friends. A nasty bout of pneumonia prevented me. From Lodz in Poland, where we were living at the time, I followed its adventure with a heavy heart.*

PARTITION OF PALESTINE INTO TWO STATES

"The war is over, but our war continues," declared David Ben Gurion. In Palestine, the Jewish resistance attacked the British occupying forces. On the Left, the Haganah, created in 1920 as a secret army, closely linked to the Labor Party, unleashed its kibbutzim commandos, the Palmach. On the Right, the Irgun, whose men blew up a wing of the King David Hotel, where the British had their headquarters, on July 22, 1946: ninety-one people were killed, most of them civilians. There was also Lehi, a breakaway group from the Irgun, known as the Stern Group, after its founder. They were well armed, and radical. In Cairo on November 6, 1944, they assassinated the British minister of state in the Middle East, Lord Moyne.

All shared the same objective: independence, but not the same methods. The Haganah regularly condemned the terrorist attacks by the Irgun and the Stern Group. British army repression, arrests, and hangings made no difference: Jewish resistance grew stronger every day. The British now began inciting Palestinian extremists to attack the kibbutzim and collective farms. They used the same methods as in India, where they encouraged Muslims to attack Hindus. In India, the situation got out of control and civil war was the result. In February 1947, unable to keep order in Palestine, the British government led by Clement Attlee decided to transfer its mandate to the United Nations. The UN Special Committee on Palestine (UNSCOP) organized the partition of Palestine into two independent states, a Jewish and an Arab one.

On November 29, 1947, the General Assembly of the United Nations adopted the Partition Plan by thirty-three votes to thirteen. The UN also enjoined Great Britain to withdraw its troops before August 1, 1948. The British reacted by arming Arab militias, beginning with the Arab Legion of Transjordan commanded by Glubb Pasha, an Englishman who had converted to Islam.

Facing page:
The King David Hotel bombing.

The attack on the King David Hotel in Jerusalem in 1946, aimed at the British occupying forces, reminds us that there was also Jewish terrorism.

Above, left:
Dayan, Sadeh, Allon (1938, Jewish National Fund, New York).

Above, right:
General Sir John Bagot Glubb, known as Glubb Pasha (c.1950).

I couldn't resist putting these two photos together. On one side, the three leaders of Palmach, the assault group made up mainly of kibbutznik: Dayan, Sadeh, and Allon; on the other, the leader of the Arab Legion, Glubb Pasha, an Englishman converted to Islam.

PROCLAMATION
OF THE STATE
OF ISRAEL

History was being made. On May 14, 1948, in front of a packed, emotional crowd at the Tel Aviv Museum, David Ben Gurion proclaimed the independence of the State of Israel. In his declaration he pledged that the state would "foster the development of the country for the benefit of all its inhabitants" and would be "based on freedom, justice, and peace as envisaged by the prophets of Israel." His text pledged "complete equality of social and political rights to all its inhabitants, irrespective of religion, race, or sex"; guaranteed "freedom of religion, conscience, language, education, and culture"; and promised to "safeguard the Holy Places of all religions" and adhere to "the principles of the Charter of the United Nations."

The first country to recognize the State of Israel was the Soviet Union. Stalin rightly considered that the independence of India and Israel would usher in the end of the colonial era and fatally weaken the British Empire. America followed the Soviet example, and then came the turn of France, other European nations, and the states of South America. Britain, however, did not consider itself defeated. Hoping that it would then be asked to intervene to restore peace, it encouraged the Arab League to fight.

THE FIRST
ARAB-ISRAELI WAR

War broke out as soon as independence was declared. The Arab armies rushed in to attack the new Israeli state. Thousands of Jewish and non-Jewish volunteers stepped forward to defend it. Syria, which occupied the northern frontier zone, retreated. The Egyptian army, in Gaza, marched on Tel Aviv. The Jewish army halted it on the road to Ashdod. Transjordan annexed what is now the West Bank, a territory set aside for the Palestinians, and part of Jerusalem.

Far left:
The first anniversary of independence (Tel Aviv, May 4, 1949).

Ben Gurion reads the declaration of independence (Tel Aviv, May 14, 1948).

Left:
I must say that I danced in Lodz, Poland, where we were living after the war, when I heard of the creation of the state of Israel. Not many people get to see a dream that is thousands of years old becoming reality.

Facing page:
The Altalena in flames (June 27, 1948, off Tel Aviv).

The day Ben Gurion imposed the same rules on all the Jewish military factions, and had the boat carrying arms commissioned by Begin and the Zionist far right blown up, that day marked the true birth of the state of Israel. I was present when Yitzhak Rabin mentioned this example to Yasser Arafat, who unfortunately failed to act on it.

Appointed as United Nations mediator in Palestine, on September 16, 1948, Count Bernadotte proposed a new partition plan with Jerusalem under international control. The next day, on September 17, 1948, he was assassinated by the Stern Group. Eventually, the United Nations stepped in. The Arabs and Israelis signed a ceasefire on February 7, 1949. What marked the true birth of the Israeli state was a bloody showdown between the Haganah, now the official Israeli army, and the Irgun.

The Irgun secretly sent a cargo ship loaded with arms into the waters off Tel Aviv. The Haganah units then appeared just as they were landing. Menachem Begin, leader of the Irgun, had bought these weapons in Europe and considered that they belonged to him. Ben Gurion replied that a state can have only one army and that Begin must give up the arms. Begin refused. Ben Gurion ordered his men to attack. Israeli soldiers sank the boat.

Eighteen men were killed in the shooting, most of them survivors of the Holocaust. The event made a deep impression. After this fratricidal confrontation, the Irgun agreed to transform itself into a political party and its fighters joined Tsahal, henceforth the one and only armed force of the State of Israel.

I myself was present when Yitzhak Rabin recounted this episode to Yasser Arafat, by way of a lesson. According to Rabin, the Palestinians could not establish an independent state without imposing a proper administration, a single authority on their many armed groups—and if necessary by force. The military coup d'état by Hamas in Gaza has proved him right.

THE ALTALENA, A FRATRICIDAL BATTLE

The first Israeli-Arab war ended in a series of armistices: with Egypt first, followed by the Rhodes Agreement of February 24, 1949, and then with Lebanon, Transjordan, and Syria between March and July. But it left scars: the massacres of Jews in Hebron and of Palestinian Arabs in the village of Deir Yassin intensified hatred on both sides. Hundreds of thousands of frightened Palestinians left their villages at the call of the Arab League, which promised that upon their victorious return they would gather booty even more sumptuous than that the Prophet collected from the Jews of Medina. Herein lies one of the main obstacles to peace between the Arab world and Israel, even today.

The proclamation of the State of Israel came as a wake-up call to most Jewish communities and caused the destruction of several of them, particularly in the Arab countries. In August 1947, in Egypt and in Tripoli, 130 Jews were killed in rioting. In December of the same year there was a pogrom in Aden—still a British protectorate at the time: eighty-two Jews were killed and hundreds of Jewish houses and shops were looted. Also in that month, the Muslim Brotherhood burned down twelve synagogues and five schools in Damascus. Most of the Syrian Jews fled to Lebanon and Turkey. In January 1952, in an anti-British demonstration in Cairo, nearly all the city's Jewish shops were pillaged and burned. Hence a new exodus by one of the world's oldest Jewish communities. In Baghdad, the dictatorship prosecuted prominent Jewish figures for spying. The Stalinist-style show trial ended with spectacular public hangings. That, too, was a very old community.

It was in this atmosphere of emergency that an airlift called On Eagles' Wings carried to Israel the mythical Jewish community of Yemen which had, over the centuries, produced a very rich body of rabbinical and poetic literature. From 1950 to 1952, Operation Ezra and Nehemiah transported twenty thousand Iraqi Jews to Israel. Iran, the only country in the Middle East to have developed friendly relations with Israel, supported the operation. But in 1979, when the Shah fell and Ayatollah Ruhollah Khomeini came to power, most of the 300,000 Jews who had been living there since time immemorial emigrated to Israel.

In May 1991 there was Operation Solomon. This time, tens of thousands of Ethiopian Jews, the Falashas, were taken to Israel. They called themselves Beta Israel, the "House of Israel," and claimed descent from the Queen of Sheba and King Solomon. Hence the name of the

Israeli troops raise their flag after taking the Jordanian base of Umm Rashrash (March 10, 1949).

Two Soviet officers were involved in the capture of the port of Eilat on the Red Sea, a port created over three thousand years earlier by King Solomon. In those days it was called Etzion Geber.

operation. In two days and eighty direct flights between Addis Ababa and Tel Aviv, fourteen thousand two hundred Ethiopian Jews reached Israel. The Ethiopian government demanded the sum of thirty-five million dollars in exchange for the authorization to emigrate.

Even so, there are still thousands of Jews in the Ethiopian province of Gondar waiting for the visa to leave. I met a few of them when I was writing a novel about the Queen of Sheba, that first black queen accepted into the pantheon of great white men. According to the oral tradition, which is an important part of the teaching there, 237 generations of kings separate Menelik, son of the Queen of Sheba and King Solomon, from Emperor Haile Selassie, the Negus of Abyssinia who was stripped of his throne by Mussolini in 1934 and assassinated in 1975 by a revolutionary dictator. According to this same tradition, Moses' Tablets of the Law are located in Ethiopia: it is said that just before he died King Solomon entrusted them to his son Menelik, who had come to be with him in Jerusalem.

The birth of Israel may have been a fillip to Jewish communities around the world, but it was fatal to some of them in the Arab world. Fleeing anti-Semitic riots, 230,000 Jews abandoned Morocco, 130,000 left Algeria and Tunisia, and 40,000 fled Libya.

The Six-Day War, in 1967, emptied the communist countries of their few remaining Jewish inhabitants.

By placing the Israeli-Arab conflict at the center of the world and of the Cold War, this war changed everything: the balance of power in the Near East, Israel's image in the world, the links between the Jewish state and the Diaspora, and, finally, relations between Jews and their compatriots.

It all began on July 26, 1956, when Gamal Abdel Nasser, who had taken power two years before at the head of a group of young, so-called progressive officers, unexpectedly nationalized the Suez Canal. In standing up against the West, the *rais* was trying to unify the Arab world against the former colonial powers and against Israel. The Soviet Union and its satellites armed and encouraged him.

The Suez Canal, that old idea of the Saint-Simonian socialists made a reality by the Frenchman Ferdinand de Lesseps, was inaugurated in 1869. One hundred and nineteen miles long, it connects the Red Sea and the Mediterranean, considerably reducing the distance between Europe and Asia. Even more importantly, it is the transport artery for oil. It is, in sun, economically vital both to the region and to the whole world.

Great Britain and France, who had been despoiled, decided to react to Nasser's act of force. The company that managed the canal belonged to them. France, Israel's main ally, asked Jerusalem for help. The Israelis agreed all the more readily because the *fedayeen*, terrorists armed by Egypt, were infiltrating its territory and making increasing numbers of attacks. Great Britain, France, and Israel therefore scattered the Egyptian army and took control of the Suez Canal. But both the United States and the Soviet Union wanted to avoid military conflict: the victors for a day were forced to withdraw. Nasser was triumphant.

Haile Selassie in front of the League of Nations (1936).

In 1936 my father Salomon helped set up a committee in support of Haile Selassie, who had been dethroned by Mussolini's fascist army. Seventy years later I traveled to Ethiopia and met the Jews of Gondar, who were still waiting for their visas to leave for Israel, but also the negus's granddaughter, Mariam Senna. I taught her a song composed in Yiddish by the Polish Jews in honor of her grandfather. History always has the last word on the gravediggers.

Les 4 sadiques agresseurs de Brigitte recherchés sur les chantiers de banlieue

(PAGE 3.)

France-Soir

dernière heure 8

Jeudi 1er juin 1967

LE SEUL QUOTIDIEN VENDANT PLUS D'UN MILLION

Belgique-Luxembourg, 3 fr. ; Suisse, 0 fr. 30 ; Espagne, 5 pesetas ; Allemagne, 50 pf. ; Italie, 80 lires ; Algérie, 0 d. al. 35 ; Maroc, 0 dirh. 40 ; Tunisie, 40 m.

L'ÉTAU DES ARMÉES ARABES SE RESSERRE SUR ISRAËL

De Gaulle chez le Pape ce matin

(PAGE 7.)

BEN BARKA : Leroy - Finville pleurait pendant la plaidoirie de son avocat

(fin du procès lundi)

(PAGE 8.)

● Michel Debré a dit à Killy et aux skieurs douaniers : « Je suis fier de vous. »

(Rubrique sportive.)

Fusillade dans un bar de Montmartre : une cliente grièvement blessée

(PAGE 9.)

Nigéria (le plus grand pays d'Afrique) : au bord de l'éclatement

(PAGE 6.)

RUE VANEAU (7ᵉ)
Seul, il met en fuite 3 gangsters

(PAGE 10.)

Cinq pages de petites annonces
● Immobilier (achat, vente, location), pages 17, 18.
● Fonds de commerce, page 18.
● Offres et demandes de situation, d'emploi, pages 14, 15, 16, 17.
● Autos, page 17.

NASSER ET HUSSEIN : ILS SE HAISSAIENT, ILS S'EMBRASSENT

Nasser donne l'accolade à Hussein qui a conservé son pistolet.

AU KIBBOUTZ, MÊME LES FEMMES ET LES ENFANTS SE PRÉPARENT A LA GUERRE

Sous l'œil d'une sentinelle attentive, les femmes et les enfants de ce village israélien participent à un exercice.

Devant plusieurs dizaines de photographes et de cameramen, Nasser et Hussein de Jordanie se sont réconciliés. Les frères ennemis se sont embrassés, effaçant leurs motifs de discorde.

TEL KAZIR (Galilée) mercredi (A.P.). — Avec une grande discipline, les femmes et les enfants d'un kibboutz (ferme collective) israélien sortent des abris après un exercice d'alerte.

En signant un pacte surprise avec Nasser, son ex-ennemi mortel, le roi de Jordanie met en danger 530 km de frontières israéliennes de plus

Il apporte à la coalition arabe une puissante armée de 50 000 hommes

Les Russes renforcent, face à la VIᵉ escadre US leur flotte de la Méditerranée avec 10 nouveaux navires dont certains lance-fusées

Cette nouvelle aggravation peut contraindre Israël à frapper vite avant la coordination entre les forces de Nasser et d'Hussein

Pages 4 et 5, les câbles des envoyés spéciaux de « France-Soir » : Alain GUINEY à Tel Aviv, Eva FOURNIER au Caire, Jean RAFFAELLI à Moscou, A. de SEGONZAC aux Nations-Unies.

Preceding pages:
Boats sunk at the entrance
to the Suez Canal at Port
Said (August 11, 1956).

Facing page:
France Soir (June 1, 1967).

Right:
Dayan (center), Yitzhak
Rabin (right), and General
Uzi Narkiss (left) in June
1967 in Jerusalem.

It is often forgotten that
the Israeli-Arab War
of 1967 was not wanted
by Israel, any more than
the conflict of 1956. We
forget the anguish of Jewish
communities around the
world and that of non-Jews
who, only twenty years after
the Shoah, were faced with
the unthinkable prospect of
another massacre of the Jews.
This makes it easier to
understand why the photo of
the three Israeli commanders
entering the old city of
Jerusalem should have been
seen all around the world.

ncouraged by this victory, which he appropriated, and proud to project himself as a great Third World leader, Nasser began to prepare his revenge. In early 1967, the Syrians attacked several Israeli villages. The Israelis riposted by shooting down six Syrian airplanes. Answering Syria's call, Nasser deployed his forces in the Sinai and demanded the withdrawal of the UN observers positioned along the border with Israel. Finally, going against international maritime law, he ordered the closure of the Strait of Tiran, making it impossible for Israel to keep out of the war. Jordan and Iraq now signed a defense pact with Egypt, and their coalition was joined by the Palestine Liberation Organization (PLO), headquartered in Gaza, which campaigned for the destruction of the State of Israel. The Arab League held an emergency meeting.

THE AWAKENING
OF ASSIMILATED JEWS

In the West, the press analyzed the opposing forces. Surely, Israel was going to be crushed. Emotions ran high: were they going to stand back and allow a second general massacre of the Jews in the same century? In the excitement of their rhetoric, Arab leaders clearly promised to drive the Israelis into the sea. Anxiety revived Jewish consciousness. All those who, in Europe and America, had moved away from community life, particularly in intellectual circles, joined the great demonstrations of solidarity with Israel. In France, for example, the philosopher Raymond Aron said, "I am what is called an 'assimilated Jew.'" He continued, "French Jews who gave their soul to all the black, brown, or yellow revolutionaries, are now howling with pain while their friends are baying for blood. I am suffering like them, with them, whatever they have said or done, not because we have become Zionists or Israelis, but because an irresistible feeling of solidarity is welling up within us. Where it comes from is not important." (***De Gaulle, Israel et les Juifs***, Plon, 1968.) Thanks to these "Jews of June 1967," the "Jewish street" was full. As for the "non-Jewish street," its support was almost total.

ISRAEL
VICTORIOUS

We know what happened next: Israel won the Six-Day War. Tsahal occupied Gaza and Sinai as well as the West Bank as far as Jordan and the Golan Heights on the Syrian side. After this surprising victory, everything changed once again. Israel's image with non-Jews was transformed. One part of opinion was full of admiration, the other—often on the Left—felt it had been manipulated. Those who had been preparing to weep for the victims were both relieved and disappointed. Solidarity changed sides: Israel now became an occupier.

While most of the Jews rejoiced at the military turnaround, they were shocked by the new image they were seeing in the eyes of the world, that of the Jew as "sure of himself and overbearing," to quote General de Gaulle's expression. Up until 1967, Israel had served as a link between communities. From 1967, it was a subject of debate and discord.

In Israel itself, the Jews experienced conflicting feelings: they were proud to have won, but often ashamed to have been transformed into occupiers, then angry when reproached for their crushing success. In communist and Arab nations, the Six-Day War gave rise to real anti-Jewish hysteria.

In the Soviet Union, fourteen years earlier, the Jews had been saved only by the death of Stalin on March 5, 1953. After the anti-Semitic trial of the "White Coats" in which Jewish doctors were accused simply because they were Jewish, Stalin had been preparing to order massive deportations when he was struck down by a cerebral hemorrhage.

SOVIET UNION:
THE CRY OF
THE "JEWS OF SILENCE"

In 1967, taking heart from Israel's victory, Russian Jews began to show signs of assertiveness. Demonstrations were held in synagogues. During the great festivals, Yom Kippur, Pesach, Simhat Torah—"rejoicing with the Torah"—the Jews came in their thousands, stopping the traffic and provoking the anger of the authorities. There were more trials. Jewish figures were accused of working with the Israeli secret services and the CIA. Some were sentenced to death, such as journalist Eduard Kuznetsov, who was tried for planning to flee the Soviet Union by hijacking an airplane. Under international pressure, his sentence was reduced to fifteen years in prison.

THE STRUGGLE
OF THE REFUSENIKS

With the first dissident movements began the saga of the "prisoners of Zion," commonly called refuseniks—those who were refused permission to emigrate. Among the best known of these was the mathematician Natan Sharansky, who later became a minister in an Israeli government. Mobilization on behalf of Soviet Jews helped patch up the bonds between communities. The Russian Nobel Prize winner played an important role in this struggle for justice. The point was not just to support the State of Israel, but also Jews who were being persecuted around the world—their right to emigrate, to express themselves freely, and to affirm their identity in countries with which they shared citizenship, a culture and often their achievements.

ISRAEL AND DIASPORA

A SUBVERSIVE PEOPLE

Top row, left to right:
Betty Friedan (August 26, 1970, New York);
Milton Friedman (March 21, 1982);
Dr. Jonas E. Salk (1955).

Bottom row, left to right:
Bob Dylan (May 24, 1971, Jerusalem);
Leonard Bernstein during a rehearsal in Copenhagen;
Irving Berlin (private collection).

The Bible says that "A good name is preferable to great wealth, favor, to silver and gold" (Proverbs, 22. 1)

Robert Oppenheimer and Albert Einstein (December 1, 1947).

I n 1989 *Life* magazine held a poll to find the hundred most famous Americans of the twentieth century: sixteen of them were Jews. Among them: Irving Berlin, Leonard Bernstein, Bob Dylan, the physicists Albert Einstein and Robert Oppenheimer, the economist Milton Friedman, the biologist Jonas Salk, and the feminist Betty Friedan.

Jews or Americans? Americans, of course. And also Jews. Albert Einstein liked to say that his knowledge came from the Diaspora, in Germany and America, and his bearings from Jerusalem.

I am sure that in Alexandria during the first century CE the proportion of famous Jews was similar. One of them, Philo, made a statement that, twenty centuries before Einstein, is comparable to his: "Alexandria is my homeland, Jerusalem my mother town." In the early twelfth century, the most important poet in Cordoba, Judah Halevi, stated that "My heart is in the East and I am at the far limits of the West."

A double identity? I hear the nationalists protest: for them, there can be no identity other than the one given by soil and blood. For them the very existence of the Jews is problematic. They refuse to allow that one can be both deeply French and deeply Jewish, English and Jewish, American and Jewish, etc. Once again, in this respect, the secular Jews are the most disconcerting: by their simple presence they prove that Judaism is not just a religion. Remember the cry of Marc Bloch before he was killed by German bullets: "*Vive la France*, long live the prophets of Israel!"

The abundance of books, studies, and symposia on the subject changes nothing: for most of our contemporaries—and for many Jews, too—the Jews and Judaism are a conundrum. Are we even capable of formulating the difference between Israelites, Jews, and Israelis? I am not sure. An Israeli is someone who has an Israeli passport. That goes without saying. But the Israelite? Someone who practices the Jewish religion? In that case, what is a Jew? And a Jew with no religion, to boot! And yet the same word is used for them all: Jews. And it seems to mean something.

Some claim that the notion of the Jewish people is a late invention, that the only real thing is the Jewish religion. That's nonsense. Unlike the Christians and Muslims, the Jews do not have a revealed religion, but a revealed Law. As for religion, their national history plays that role for them. Thus, over the centuries, those who adhered to Judaism as a religion automatically identified with the ancestral history of the Jewish people. It is the same for their national claims. Do they not agree to repeat, with all the other Jews scattered around the world, "Next year in Jerusalem"?

It now becomes easier to understand the difficulties of Jewish historiography. All the more so since, unlike that of other peoples, the history of the Jews, with its mixture of facts and myths, has no unity of place. Each new event modifies and enriches the meaning of an ancient event. Hence the importance and inevitable arbitrariness of the choice that is made from the abundance of possible narratives, especially as we approach our own times and events come thick and fast, if only because of the previously inconceivable circulation of information.

Rembrandt, Philo the Jew (1635, Bibliothèque Nationale, Paris).

I feel real affection for Philo. Because of his writings, of course, but most of all because of his courage in personally taking a petition to Caligula protesting the persecution of the Jews of Alexandria. That was in the year 43 CE —he was already doing what we intellectuals do now.

n Rijn in

PHILON LE JUIF

F. L. D. Ciartres excu

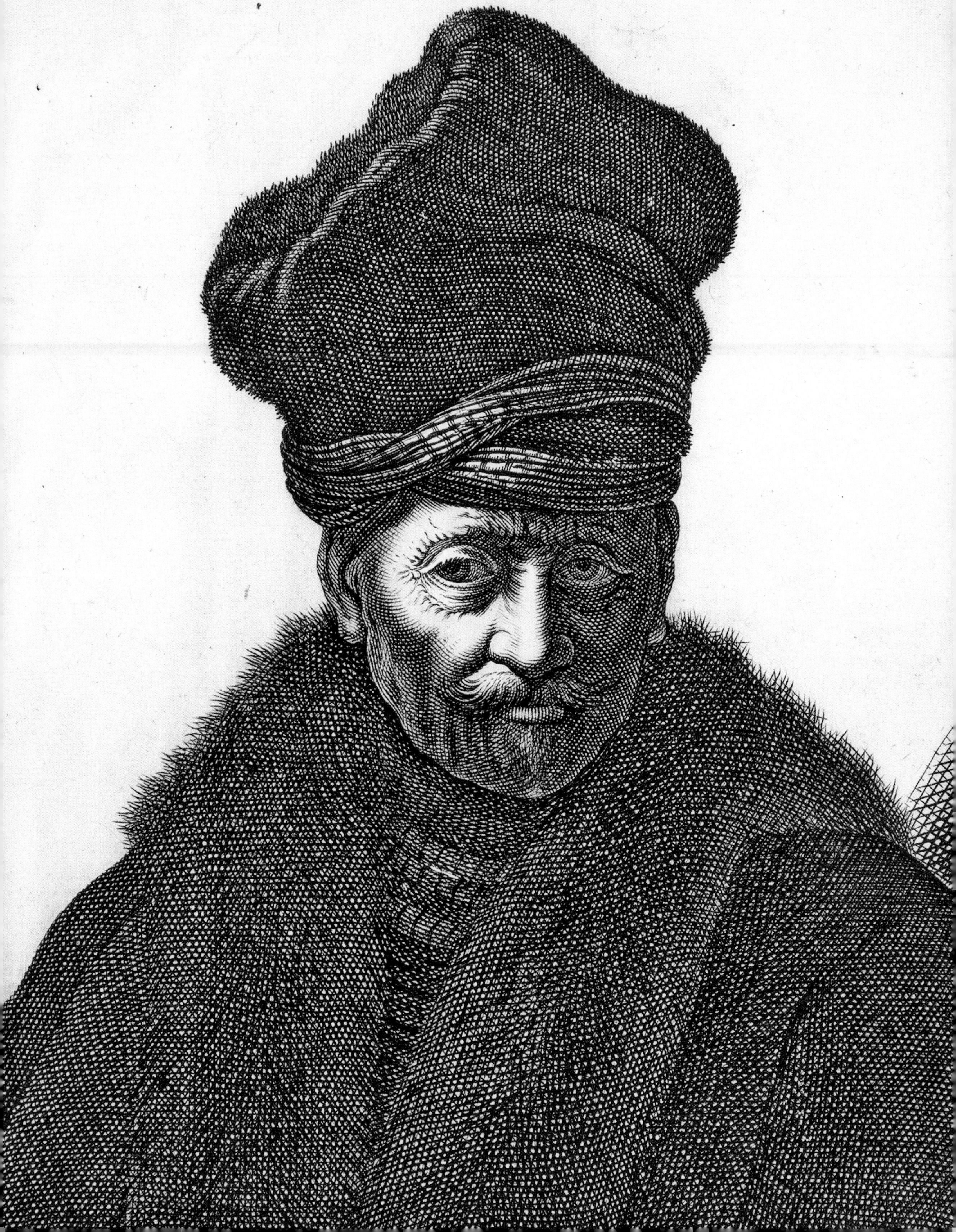

But before I continue, a few words about the distribution of the Jewish people in the contemporary world. It is generally thought that there are fourteen million Jews in the world. This is an approximate figure. In democratic countries censuses involving ethnic or religious criteria are prohibited; in totalitarian countries, such accounting, if it exists, is used merely to pave the way for or accompany persecution, as was seen in communist Poland in the late 1960s. So, according to estimates, there are over fourteen million Jews in the world: a drop in the ocean of seven billion human beings.

THE JEWS
IN THE UNITED
STATES

After the extermination of European Judaism by the Nazis, the heart of the Diaspora was now in the United States. There, the Jews were living the dream of their European brothers: playing a full role in society without forsaking any of their specific identity.

The exilarch, or Reish Galuta in Aramaic, is the leader of Jewish communities in exile, a function invented in Babylon in the second century BCE. Today, he is based in America: for one thing, because that is the home of the biggest Jewish community, (nearly six million people)—bigger even than that of Israel, (where 20 percent of the seven million inhabitants are Arabs). And, for another, because the biggest American organizations, such as B'nai B'rith/the Anti Defamation League, the American Jewish Committee, and the World Jewish Congress, are the only ones capable of stimulating, coordinating, and, if necessary, financing the activity of Jewish communities around the world.

In 1825 Mardocaï Manuel Noah, an American Jewish writer of Portuguese ancestry, dreamed of establishing a Jewish refuge and bought Grand Island in the Niagara River. There, in front of a crowd of cheering friends, he laid the first stone of a town that he called Ararat—for the mountain (located between Turkey and Armenia) where it is said that, thousands of years ago, Noah and his family emerged from the ark in which God had protected them from the flood. Talk about symbolism!

Now, it was the whole of the United States that had become a Mount Ararat: a refuge from the Holocaust for those Jews who were able to escape there.

THE JEWS
IN FRANCE

In France there are reportedly over six hundred thousand Jews, both Ashkenazim and Sephardim. The former are a mixture of descendants of communities that settled in France centuries ago and emigrants from Central Europe. Most of the Sephardim arrived between 1956,

the year of Moroccan and Tunisian independence, and 1967, the year of the Six-Day War, which emptied North Africa of its remaining Jews. To this figure we can add the tens of thousands of Jews who came to France in 1962, after the Algerian proclamation of independence.

La Ghriba synagogue, Djerba.
This is one of the oldest synagogues in the Mediterranean area. Jewish places of worship suffered less in the East than in the West.

LARGE JEWISH COMMUNITIES

There are said to be 450,000 Jews in Canada and slightly fewer in the United Kingdom. In the 1960s, in Argentina, before the rise of the military regime with its policy of repression tinged with anti-Semitism, there were 350,000 Jews. Some of them emigrated to Israel, others to the United States and Spain. It is estimated that something over 200,000 remain there today. In Australia there are 150,000 Jews, in Brazil nearly 120,000, and in South Africa nearly 90,000. In Hungary there are still 55,000, as there are in Mexico. In Belgium there are 40,000 and in Germany, particularly Berlin, where there is a large community of Russian Jews, they are close to 100,000.

THE JEWS
IN RUSSIA
TODAY

As for Russia itself, it is an enigma. It is said to have 300,000 Jews, including the 85,000 in Ukraine. Russian officials give the figure of one million. Before perestroika, when the refuseniks were fighting for the right to emigrate to Israel, there were, according to Elie Wiesel's famous book *The Jews of Silence*, 1.75 million Jews in the USSR. Since then, most of them have left for Israel. Others emigrated to the United States, where Brooklyn grew its own Little Odessa. So who are the 300,000 Jews mentioned by Jewish organizations? And what of the figure of one million put forward by the authorities? Many are the children of assimilated families or mixed couples who, in a sprit of opposition or self-affirmation, lay claim to their Jewishness.

Of course, we should not forget the 35,000 Italian Jews, the 25,000 Dutch Jews and the 18,000 Swiss Jews, and above all the 25,000 Jews of Iran, heirs to the ancient community mentioned by the Book of Esther, which is read every year during the holiday of Purim. They are alluded to in the deuterocanonical texts of the Alexandria Septuagint, the first transcription of the Bible into Greek, which has served as a matrix for all the world's other translations.

There are three expressions that can be used for Jews not living in Israel: *diaspora*, a Greek word which means dispersion and puts all Jews, wherever they live, on the same level; *galut*, a Hebrew word for exile, which accords primacy to the Jews of Israel and implies that the others all live in the expectation of return; and finally, *sherit Israel*, a Hebrew term that can be translated as "remnant of Israel," a concept invented by the prophets. This last expression refers to hidden or forgotten Jewish communities that continue to preserve their core memories, to keep the embers alive under the ashes. Thanks to them, in periods of crisis the fire can be fanned back to life and contribute to the renaissance of their people.

Facing page:
N. Jay Jaffee, Morris Meat Market (1951, Brooklyn Museum of Art, New York).

In the United States everyone arrives with their own language and, unlike Europe, where double identity is an issue, a few words of English are enough to make you an American. That doesn't prevent people from thinking of themselves as Jews, and showing it.

Right:
The Mausoleum of Esther and Mordecai, no doubt the tomb of the Jewish wife of the Sassanid king Yazdegerd (1978, Hamadan, Iran).

For all his anti-Jewish rants, the Iranian president, Ahmadinejad, cannot change historical facts: it was thanks to the Persians that the Jews were able to rebuild the Temple of Jerusalem after it was destroyed by Babylon, and also thanks to the Persians that they regained independence in the fourth century BCE.

When did the Jews reach China? It is impossible to say with any certainty. The first written evidence of their presence dates from the eighth century. In those days they were living in Hangzhou, Ningbo, and Kaifeng, in modern-day Henan province. Only the inhabitants of Kaifeng are still able to remember them. Men and women who consider themselves to be descendants ensure they are not forgotten: the American novelist and Nobel Prize laureate Pearl Buck paid them a moving tribute in her book *Peony* (1948). In addition to these recollections and letters from travelers such as Benjamin of Tudela who, between 1165 and 1173, visited most of the Jewish communities around the world, stone stelae dating from the fifteenth, sixteenth, and seventeenth centuries were found in the courtyard of the synagogue in Kaifeng, bearing inscriptions in Chinese.

It is thought that Jewish merchants, most of them from Persia, came to the region under the Song dynasty (960–1279). In those days Kaifeng was the capital of China and a major center of trade. The first synagogue built in the Chinese style was erected in 1163. It was swept away by the flooding Huang He, or Yellow River, and rebuilt in the fifteenth century.

In 1605 the mandarin Ai Tian, a Jew from Kaifeng, traveled to Beijing. They told him that the Jesuit father Matteo Ricci was in the city. A monotheist? Ai Tian assumed that this meant he was a coreligionist who had come from the Holy Land. He decided to go and see him. They met in the Jesuit church, which the Jews took to be a synagogue. This was how the Jesuits of Beijing discovered the existence of flourishing Jewish communities in China and conveyed the news to Rome.

Finally, in the eighteenth century, when the first European Jews came to Kaifeng, members of the community there were still going to the synagogue for the three daily prayers, although they no longer spoke Hebrew. They followed the laws of *kashrut* and kept the Shabbat and the Jewish festivals. Physically, they were no different from their neighbors. They dressed like the Chinese, wore pigtails, bound the feet of their daughters, and practiced the same professions—farmer, shopkeeper, craftsmen, scholar, soldier, or doctor.

At the end of the Ming dynasty the synagogue at Kaifeng burned down and was rebuilt twenty years later. In 1810 the last rabbi of Kaifeng died. The scrolls of the Torah became simple objects of veneration that nobody could decipher.

開封猶太國人攝影 民國三十八年午月秋中日

Group of Chinese Jews in front of the cathedral at Kaifeng; David Levy (far right), known as Mr. Wong (August 1924, Museum of the Jewish People, Tel-Aviv).

A surprising image, this: a group of Chinese Jews accompanied by a priest and a rabbi. My grandfather Abraham would have exclaimed, "Look how far Judaism has come!"

China never took any discriminatory measures against its Jews, and some of them even reached high office. In private, Zhou Enlai used to say that his ancestors were Jews from Kaifeng. Even today, several Chinese scientists and generals acknowledge this surprising and moving ancestry.

Between 1946 and 1948, as Mao Zedong's Red Army was propelling the Communists to power, the Jews began leaving Shanghai for the United States, Australia, and Israel. A few hundred stayed behind. The city's synagogue was still full on holy days. Originally formed by Jews from Baghdad, this community had also welcomed Russian Jews fleeing the country's new regime after the Bolshevik revolution.

THE JEWS
IN JAPAN

And what of the Jews in Japan? Here is another example of the complexity of Jewish history. Their story begins in Vilnius, known in those days as "the Lithuanian Jerusalem," at the start of World War II. The city had a dozen highly renowned rabbinical schools, or yeshivas. As the German army approached, the students and their rabbi teachers tried to escape into the USSR. The Soviets refused them entry. Caught between the Nazis and the Russians, they knocked at all the consulate doors. Everyone turned them away, except the Japanese consul, Sempo Sugihara, who was moved by the plight of these men and women and granted them visas. Thus several thousand Jews from Vilnius were able to cross Russia, all the way to Vladivostok, and sail for Japan: fleeing collectively on the Trans-Siberian. Unfortunately, on December 7, 1941, the day before they arrived, the Japanese army attacked Pearl Harbor. At the same moment, a Wehrmacht delegation arrived in Tokyo to try to work out a joint military strategy. Overtaken by events, the Japanese sent the Lithuanian Jews to Shanghai, which was under their control. There they were taken in by the local community. However, to please their German allies, the Japanese soon confined them to the Hongkou district, which became a ghetto.

THE JEWS
IN INDIA

No account of the Diaspora would be complete without the Jews of India. The Bible tells us that around 969 BCE, with the help of the Phoenician king Hiram of Tyre, King Solomon had ships built in the old Red Sea port of Ezion-Geber. It is believed that some of these boats sailed as far as India. Was this the origin of the first Jewish communities on the subcontinent? The Book of Esther (1:1 and 8:9) and the First Book of the Maccabees both mention the presence of Jews in Hoddu, India. Traces have been found of a Jewish community living in Cranganore (Kodungallur) on the Malabar Coast in the first century BCE. The Hindu kings treated the community with respect and even gave them a territory known by the name of Anjuvannam, said at the time to be the only Jewish land outside Israel. In 1524 Muslims attacked the Jews of Cranganore, who took refuge in Cochin (now part of Kerala). There the rajah guaranteed them protection and settled them in a town near his capital. This community survived occupation by the Portuguese (1500–1663), Dutch (1663–1795), and British (1795–1948), and celebrated Indian independence alongside the Hindus.

Jewish family in India (c.1890, Museum of the Jewish People, Tel Aviv).

What makes these Indians Jews? Because they want to be. Being free to choose what one is: what a joy!

THE BENE ISRAEL

There is another Jewish community that developed in and around Mumbai: the Bene Israel, or "Children of Israel." According to legend, its members are descended from the ten tribes that were scattered around the world by the Assyrian king Tiglath-Pileser III in 722 BCE. These exiles tried to reach the community at Cranganore but it would seem that their ships were carried toward Mumbai and Alibag. The name Bene Israel tends to suggest that they arrived in India between 722 and 586 BCE, before the word *Yehudim* came into use to designate the Jews.

The Bene Israel quickly learned Marathi, the Indo-European language of the Mumbai region. This is why some historians believed they were Hindus who had converted to Judaism. Not at all. Although isolated, the Bene Israel kept the essential parts of Judaism; they read the Torah in Marathi. When the State of Israel was created some of them emigrated, as indeed did nearly all the Jews of Cochin.

There are still Bene Israel communities in Mumbai and New Delhi today. They speak Hindi, but they still pray in Hebrew.

Preceding pages:
The Israeli Army in the Sinai Desert (October 1973).

What does war—even a defensive war—ever leave? Memorials and photographs. And sometimes very beautiful ones.

Left:
Moshe Dayan and Golda Meir (July 26, 1972).

Men make history, and then history, like carbon paper, records them or erases them from its events. Here are two significant figures from the history of Israel whose image was blemished by the Yom Kippur War in 1973. I was very fond of Golda Meir. For me, she was a bit like the grandmother I wasn't lucky enough to know.

Facing page:
Menachem Begin and Shimon Peres in a televised debate (1977).

Wanted poster for Menachem Begin (1947). Two Israels go head to head on the television screen, proving the "normalization" of a state that managed to transform its "terrorists" into responsible politicians.

THE YOM
KIPPUR WAR

But let us come back to Israel and the shock of 1973: the Yom Kippur War, when Egypt and Syria launched a surprise attack on Israel and pushed it to the brink of disaster. Because of the resounding victory of the Six-Day War, people had forgotten the precariousness that defines the condition of the Jewish people. The Arab advance in the first days of October 1973 was a powerful reminder of the threat that had hung over them for thousands of years.

The biblical prophets would have interpreted the Yom Kippur War as a warning: improvidence and contempt for the adversary. "Where there is no vision, the people get out of hand" (Proverbs 29:18).

After the Six-Day War, the Israeli army had retreated behind supposedly impregnable fortifications built along the eastern bank of the Suez Canal, the Bar-Lev Line, named after the Israeli chief of staff who built it. For the prime minister Golda Meir, and Moshe Dayan, the defense minister, it seemed obvious that the Arabs were incapable of matching Israel, and would be for years to come. When the Egyptian president Anwar el-Sadat launched his divisions across the Suez Canal on October 6, 1973, in the middle of Yom Kippur, the Day of Atonement—or of Ramadan for Muslims—the Israelis were taken totally by surprise. All the more since the Syrians, Egypt's allies, simultaneously attacked Israel's positions in the Golan Heights.

Tsahal, the Israeli army, rallied quickly. General Sharon's Armored Division outflanked the Third Egyptian Army in the Sinai, crossed the Suez Canal near the Great Bitter Lake, and entered Egypt. However, Sharon had to halt his advance: on a decision by Secretary of State Henry Kissinger, the United States had suspended delivery of the parts needed for his American-made tanks.

Militarily, once again, Israel had come out of it well. Politically, however, Sadat had won the war. For the Arabs, he had shattered the myth of Tsahal's invincibility. This won him glory in the Third World. A few years later, this meant he could negotiate with yesterday's enemy without losing face. On top of this considerable shift, the Yom Kippur War radically changed Israel's political life. To sum up: if the Six-Day War transformed the image of the Diaspora Jews, the Yom Kippur War changed the image of Israel.

Ever since Theodor Herzl and his book *The Jewish State*, Zionists had held that Israel should be an exemplary state. This idea had motivated the generations of pioneers, most of them on the Left, who forged an Israeli society whose heart was the kibbutz—the collective farm, provider of the military and intellectual elite—and whose body was the Histadrut, the General Federation of Labor. This union organization controlled every aspect of daily life. It was the upholders of this brand of Zionism who were at the head of the state when the Yom Kippur War broke out. After the narrowly averted disaster the population withdrew its confidence in them. Israeli society had changed. The children of the pioneers from Europe had been joined by Sephardic communities who claimed to know the Arab world after centuries of living in it. They contested the more idealistic vision of the European Jews then in power. In rejecting the political class, these newer Israelis also abandoned its values and its socialist and social ideology. Fleeing Arab totalitarianism, they had little notion of democracy and believed in strength. They were now the majority. Their vote in the 1977 election brought about what can be considered a political sea change. Having held power ever since independence, the Labor Party now had to abandon government to the nationalist Right, the Herut—today's Likud—led by Menachem Begin, the sworn enemy of Ben Gurion since 1948. To the despair of many Jewish intellectuals around the world who saw Israel's Jewish particularism as the chief obstacle to its integration in the Middle East, the Jewish State lost some of its dream and gained in normality.

On November 19, 1977, the Egyptian president Anwar el-Sadat took the very courageous initiative of announcing his intention to visit Israel. In the morning he arrived in his white airplane at Tel Aviv's Ben Gurion Airport; the same evening, he was in Jerusalem speaking to the Israelis from the Knesset. The peace process had been set in motion. The Egypt-Israel peace treaty was signed on March 26, 1979, in Washington.

ANWAR EL-SADAT IN ISRAEL

But the enemies of peace were vigilant. On October 6, 1981, at the parade commemorating the Yom Kippur War, members of Tanzim al-Jihad (Egyptian Islamic Jihad), a radical offshoot of the Islamic Brotherhood, assassinated Anwar el-Sadat in Cairo. In keeping with the Camp David Agreement, and despite strong resistance by Jewish extremists, the Israeli prime minister, Menachem Begin, continued with the withdrawal from Sinai. Similar protests and scenes were witnessed when Ariel Sharon began dismantling the colonies in Gaza in 2005.

THE ASSASSINATION OF SADAT

In the 1980s and 1990s Israeli society leaned to the Right. So did the Diaspora, and so indeed did the West as a whole: "In the Jewish Street as in the Christian Street" goes the old Yiddish adage. This was a logical reaction to the visible failure and final fall of communism. But the weakening of the Left also undermined the secular ideal. As it receded, so religious schools burgeoned among the Jews, Muslims, and Christians.

In the United States this religious wave was channeled by the Hasidic movement. As in Central Europe before the war, it formed around a few renowned rabbis supported by their often wealthy disciples. Their influence was immense, even on American politics.

THE RETURN OF THE RELIGIOUS

The most dynamic element within this Hasidic Judaism was—and is—the Lubavitch movement. Founded in Belarus in the eighteenth century by Rabbi Shneur Zalman of Liadi, it put the emphasis on good works, kabbalah, and study. In those days it was called Chabad, an acronym combining letters from the three kabbalistic values of wisdom, understanding, and knowledge. The descendants of Shneur Zalman of Liadi settled in the village of Lyubavichi, from the Russian for love: *lubov*. It stood near the Berezina, a river now synonymous with the debacle of Napoleon's retreat from Moscow.

Rabbi Joseph Yitzhak Schneersohn (1880–1950) was a superb organizer. Before World War II he set up an impressive network of Chabad communities across Europe, commonly known as the

THE LUBAVITCH MOVEMENT

Lubavitch. Seeing the Nazi danger, he emigrated to the United States and settled in Brooklyn. His home, at 770 Eastern Parkway, became known as simply "770." Oddly enough, the movement attracted many members with a university background. Soon Rabbi Joseph Yitzhak had covered the United States with a network of religious schools and institutions. The success of the Lubavitch would become emblematic of the new vigor of religious Judaism in the late twentieth century.

Menachem Mendel Schneersohn, with whom I had conversations in French and Yiddish—he had studied at the Sorbonne—succeeded him at the head of the Lubavitch movement. Tens of thousands made the pilgrimage to Brooklyn to meet him. Until his death in 1994, no American presidential candidate dared to stand without the rabbi's benediction. A stocky figure which a big white beard and wrinkled, dark eyes looking out alertly from under his big black hat, he received visitors flanked by two burly Jewish beadles in long coats and black hats.

To each one he would give a five-dollar note. When I told the rabbi that I found this surprising mixture of mystical fervor and money rather shocking, he took me out into the street and gestured towards the dozens of beggars sitting along the wall. "Many of the people who come to see me don't even have a dollar to give alms to the poor. When they walk past these homeless people they feel uncomfortable. Because of the money I give them they are able to do a good deed." In 1980, when the Israeli pacifist movement took the name Peace Now, the Lubavitch launched the slogan *Mechiah Now*— "the Messiah Now." In the end, though, isn't that the same thing?

The Lubavitch do not have a monopoly on Jewish religious practice. This has three main tendencies: the Orthodox, the Conservative, and the Reform Jews.

Preceding pages:
Hasidic Jews in the synagogue at Crown Heights (New York).

Pretty impressive, this assembly of Hasidim, don't you think?

Left:
Rabbi Menachem, Mendel Schneerson (New York).

Menachem Mendel Schneerson used to hand his visitors dollar notes so that they could give them as alms to the poor who gathered round his home. I must confess to having taken two and kept one for luck.

Facing page:
Isaac Mayer Wise.

Reform Judaism, a response to Orthodox Judaism. Richness lies in diversity.

Orthodox Judaism appeared in around 1795 during the Haskala, the emancipation. It stands for traditional practices and beliefs, in opposition to the innovations put forward by the Reform Jews. Orthodox Jews invoke the Law inspired by God and are strict in following the teachings of the Halacha (from the verb *halakh*, to walk). "Your task is to ... teach them the statutes and laws, and show them the way they ought to follow and how they ought to behave" (Exodus 18:19–20). In the United States, it is the Yeshiva University of New York that constitutes the main intellectual center of Orthodox Judaism.

ORTHODOX
JUDAISM

Conservative Judaism, or *Masorti*, emerged in Europe in the nineteenth century, in the period following emancipation. The dominant tendency in the United States, it seeks to chart a middle course between the "rigidity" of Orthodoxy and the "indulgence" of Reform. Conservative Judaism is sustained by the Jewish Theological Seminary of America, founded in New York in 1886. It sees rationalism as a key principle of Jewish thought. It limits Hebrew to liturgical use and attenuates a number of significant rules: for example, it accepts that Jewishness can be passed on by the father, and not just the mother, dispenses with a blessing that is humiliating for women, and evokes the Holocaust in its prayers. Its followers also tend to be committed Zionists.

CONSERVATIVE
JUDAISM

As for Reform Judaism, it denies the immutability of the written law and seeks to adapt Jewish thought and practice to the spirit of the age. The first Reform community in the United States was founded in Albany in 1846 by Rabbi Isaac Mayer Wise, who was born in Prague in 1819. It soon spread from his congregation to become the majority tendency. In 1873 Wise inaugurated the Union of American Hebrew Congregations and in 1875 he opened the Hebrew Union College, the first seminary for Reform rabbis, in Cincinnati. Reform Jews introduced mixed choirs and congregations as well as religious confirmation for young girls. Liberal and Progressive Judaism both derive from this trend.

REFORM
JUDAISM

The movement originated in Germany. In 1818 its founders opened a Reform temple in Hamburg. Already, they were using a modified book of prayer. "Only the ethical laws of the Torah still have binding values for Jews," is their position. Reform Jews publish the *Union Prayer Book*. Their practice is limited to a weekly service based around a sermon given by the rabbi. Consequently the architecture of Reform synagogues makes the pulpit the central element. Religious instruction for children is provided by Sunday school.

In adapting to the modern world, these currents of Judaism sought to open up to young people, particularly in America. At the same time the Christian world—starting with the Catholics—has changed its attitude toward the Jews. Much has changed since the silence of Pius XII over the Holocaust, so controversially decried by the German writer Rolf Hochhuth in his play *The Deputy*, which premiered in West Berlin on August 20, 1963. In Vatican II and the *Nostra aetate* declaration of 1965, the Church officially ceased to designate the Jews as a deicide people and openly condemned anti-Semitism.

Then came John Paul II, Karol Jozef Wojtyla: the 264th pope, and the first to come from Central Europe. He was also the first pope for whom a Jew was not a controversial abstraction but a human being of flesh and blood—a neighbor, sometimes a friend, a person involved in the same spiritual adventure as a Christian, but even older. A Pole, Karol Wojtyla was born in 1920 near Cracow. Two-thirds of the people in his village, Wadowice, were Jews, and he witnessed their massacre in World War II. He lived with a feeling of guilt. His attachment to that lost world—his own world, too—and his inability to save it marked the whole of his papacy. His visit to the Great Synagogue (Tempio Maggiore) in Rome on April 13, 1986, was even more memorable than his trip to Israel, following that of Pope Paul VI, for this was the first time a head of the Church had visited a Jewish place of worship since Saint Paul himself. John Paul's speech, "You are our beloved brothers, our older brothers," signaled a radical change in the relations between Jews and Christians. On June 15, 1994, the Vatican established diplomatic relations with the State of Israel.

So, everything is fine? No. A new wind cannot blow away two millennia of hate. Even if knowledge can help men rid themselves of certain prejudices, man does not change overnight. At the very moment when, spurred on by Pope John Paul II, the Polish episcopate was, in all its churches, reading out a pastoral letter of friendship for the Jews, "this people to whom God revealed His name and with whom he passed a covenant," in France an extremist group was profaning the Jewish cemetery in Carpentras. A reminder that anti-Semitism, whose stench Jews had begun to forget, had not simply disappeared.

CHRISTIANS AND JEWS: THE NEW SITUATION

CARPENTRAS, THE LIFTING OF A TABOO

What happened? On the night of May 8–9, 1990, unidentified individuals dug up the recently buried corpse of Félix Germon and staged a fake impaling. This profanation could have been no more than a sordid crime, but it occurred at a moment when the guilty conscience governing relations between Jews and non-Jews since the Holocaust was beginning to recede, especially among the generations born after the war. The profanation of the cemetery in Carpentras marked the lifting of a taboo, the end of the restraint toward the Jews that the West had imposed on itself since 1945.

In Paris several hundreds of thousands of people took to the streets. At the head of this impressive demonstration was the clergy, around the primate of the French Church, Monsignor Decourtray. François Mitterrand, the president of France, had been informed of the event's magnitude and came to meet the demonstrators. At the top of boulevard Beaumarchais, the dense crowd moving toward place de la Bastille joined the thousand or so people accompanying the president. Cardinal Jean-Marie Lustiger, who was Archbishop of Paris at the time and, himself a Jew by birth, was marching at my side; he was moved to tears. I remarked to him that he was seeing the last great demonstration of solidarity with the Jews. Unfortunately, I was right. The spirit of sympathy that had prevailed from the end of the war to the 1990s had evaporated. The Jews returned to "normality": uncertainty and vulnerability.

ANTI-SEMITIC ACTS AND THE RESURGENT FAR RIGHT

May 9, 1990: profanation of the Jewish cemetery in Carpentras. April 21, 2002: Jean-Marie Le Pen, the candidate of the Front National, France's nationalist, anti-Semitic Right, reached the second round of the presidential election. This moral errancy, this wavering of public opinion on the Jewish question, was not limited to France.

On August 19, 1991, an African American killed a religious Jewish student in the first interethnic riot witnessed in Crown Heights, New York. In October of the same year, again in the United States, the Nation of Islam movement accused the Jews of having organized, financed, and controlled the slave trade. A historical absurdity. On July 18, 1994, a bomb exploded at the Asociación Mutual Israelita Argentina, a Jewish community center in Buenos Aires, killing eighty-five people. Argentinean anti-Semites accused the Jews of causing the attack in order to exert pressure on the government. On February 24, 1995, neo-Nazis held their first

demonstration in Berlin. On December 14, the anti-Semitic Liberal Democratic Party of Vladimir Zhirinovsky won fifty-one seats in the Duma, the Russian parliament. On June 13, 1999, in Belgium, the Vlaams Blok—now the Flemish Vlaams Belang—a racist and anti-Semitic movement, came third in the Flemish parliamentary elections with 9.9 percent of the vote. On October 14 of the same year, in Austria, the fascistic Freiheitlichen Partei Österreichs led by Jörg Haider came second in the legislative elections with 26.91 percent of the vote. On October 24 in Switzerland, the Schweizerische Volkspartei, led by far-right politician Christoph Blocher, was the second biggest group in the National Council with 22 percent of the votes. Finally, on November 30, several Swedish newspapers revealed the existence of a large anti-Semitic network in the country.

Facing page:
Riot at Crown Heights, New York (1991).

Above, left:
After the explosion at the Asociación Mutual Israelita Argentina in Buenos Aires (July 18, 1994).

Above, right:
Louis Farrakhan, leader of the Nation of Islam movement (April 11,1984).

It is symptomatic that, whatever their religious, political, or national identity, all enemies of the Jews are one in their hatred—the hatred that makes them feel they exist.

Perhaps only Britain was spared—notwithstanding the revisionist writings of the historian David Irving. Irving lost his court case against the American historian Deborah Lipstadt, who had denounced the racism of his arguments. The British Jewish community, which is represented by a very ancient institution, the Board of Deputies, publishes a weekly newspaper founded in 1841, the *Jewish Chronicle*, the influence of which reaches far beyond Jewish circles. The Jewish community is proud to have given Britain six Nobel prizewinners: Max Perutz (chemistry), Bernard Katz and César Milstein (medicine), Brian Josephson and Dennis Gabor (physics), and Harold Pinter (literature).

Elsewhere, in countries where there were no more Jews, such as Poland or Japan, the years from 2000 to 2002 saw record numbers of anti-Semitic acts. A small note of hope in this dark period was sounded when Jacques Chirac, president of France, recognized French responsibility in the deportation of the Jews under Vichy. His predecessor François Mitterrand had doggedly refused to make this gesture. On July 16, 1995, at the ceremony commemorating the Vélodrome d'Hiver roundup, when over thirteen thousand Jews were deported with the help of the French police, Jacques Chirac declared: "On that day France, homeland of the Enlightenment and of human rights, land of refuge and asylum, did what can never be repaired."

The Vel d'Hiv roundup (July 16, 1942, Paris).

These men and women, brought here by Frenchmen, are doomed to die. But let us not forget the Righteous, by whose efforts, in France, more than two thirds of the community survived the war.

Why this monstrous regression? After all, the 1990s had got off to a good start. In Israel, on March 18, 1992, the Knesset instituted election of the prime minister by universal suffrage. On June 23, the Labor Party leader Yitzhak Rabin, who had been chief of staff during the Six-Day War, came to power. On September 13, the world witnessed the inconceivable: Rabin and Arafat shaking hands on the steps of the White House in Washington, in front of a satisfied-looking Bill Clinton. At the same time, after nine months of discussion at Borregaard, outside the Norwegian capital, the two negotiators, Mahmoud Abbas, Arafat's second in command, and Shimon Peres, the Israeli Foreign Minister, signed the official document known as the Oslo Accords.

But then, on November 4, 1995, after a peace rally on Kings of Israel Square in Tel Aviv, an Israeli extremist, the religious student Yigal Amir, shot Yitzhak Rabin at point-blank range.

In Israel and in the Diaspora, and for all those hoping for peace, the murder of the Israeli prime minister was a disaster. It was, however, a relief for the minority who believed that Rabin had made too many concessions to Arafat. Subsequent attempts to revive the peace process—at Wye Plantation in 1998, at Sharm el-Sheikh in 1999, at Camp David in 2000, and at Taba in 2001—all ended in failure. The Palestinian cause became increasingly dear to the world, and not least to its many anti-Semitic movements.

In four thousand years of Jewish history, only one precedent can be found for the assassination of Yitzhak Rabin: the killing of Gedaliah, governor of Judaea in 586 BCE. When large numbers of Judaeans went into exile in Babylon, having been deported by Nebuchadnezzar, the king left Gedaliah ben Ahikam to govern Judah in his name. A strong, realistic man, Gedaliah was accused of selling the country to foreigners and was assassinated by one Ishmael ben Netanyah. Shocked by the crime and encouraged by the prophet Jeremiah, the people instituted a fast in memory of the executed governor, the fast of Gedaliah, held the day after the Jewish New Year. It is still observed today.

ידיעות אחרונות

Yedioth Ahronoth · یدیعوت اهرونوت

רצח רבין: העדות ההיסטורית

"ידיעות אחרונות" מפרסם היום פירסום בלעדי ראשון של צילומי רצח ראש הממשלה, מתוך סרט־הוידאו שתיעד את הטרגדיה ● הסרט ישודר הערב ב־8 בחדשות ערוץ 2

השנייה שבה נרצח ראש ממשלת ישראל: יגאל עמיר (מימין, מסומן בחץ) מתקרב למרחק של סנטימטרים ספורים מיצחק רבין, מושיט את ידו - יורה על ראש הממשלה (באמצע, מסומן בחץ). מאחורי גבו של ראש הממשלה נראה הרשל של יריית האקדח. משמאלו של רבין (צמוד אליו, בעניבה) - המאבטח יורם רובין, שנפצע מאחד מכדורי המתנקש. בין יגאל עמיר ליצחק רבין ניצב הסטודנט ישראל מרדי לתקשורת, שהתקרב לראש הממשלה בניסיון לראיין אותו. (תצלום: רוני קמפלר)

התר לפרסום: 3 מרגלים לטובת סוריה בכלא בישראל

נלכדו בשנת 1993 ונדונו ל־6 עד 8.5 שנים עירעורם לעליון נדחה · עמ' 23

משפטו של יגאל עמיר נפתח הבוקר בבית המשפט המחוזי בת"א

כתב האישום ייקרא בפניו - והוא יאמר לשופטים: מודה או לא מודה · עמ' 21

ראש השב"כ לא יתפטר בעקבות מכתב האזהרה מוועדת שמגר

הוועדה שיגרה מכתבי אזהרה ל־6 מראשי השירות ולבכיר במשטרה · עמוד 20

But what day of fasting, what commemoration followed Rabin's death? None. Why? Are today's Jews less sensitive than their ancestors to the pedagogical virtues of their own history? If you cease to see history as a lesson, it can end up teaching you one. On September 28, 2000, Ehud Barak, leader of the Labor Party and prime minister, authorized his political adversary, General Sharon, to go to Temple Mount, the Muslim Noble Sanctuary. The Palestinians took this as an act of political provocation. Seven Palestinians were killed in ensuing clashes between demonstrators and police. Thus began the second Intifada, the "war of stones" against the Israelis.

We think monotheism has triumphed over polytheism, but in reality this is the reign of paganism. History is reduced to a set of images. Palestinian teenagers attacking the Israeli army with stones immediately conjures up the image of David confronting Goliath the Philistine with his sling: in the eyes of television viewers, justice has changed sides.

"We are the Jews of the Near East," Yasser Arafat said to me one day. I replied that he was right to call for a Palestinian state, but that this did not make him a Jew. To be a Jew, you had to have centuries of persecution behind you—something I certainly wouldn't wish on him. I also told him that the Palestinians were certainly lucky to be fighting the Jews. Arafat was surprised. He asked me why. I explained that if they'd had to fight another enemy, whoever it might be, almost nobody would have talked about them.

Unfortunately, it is not the Palestinian cause that mobilizes public opinion so much as hatred of Israel. The Kurds, for example, have been fighting for independence much longer than the Palestinians. No one talks about them.

IF YOU CEASE
TO SEE HISTORY
AS A LESSON, IT WILL
TEACH YOU ONE

WHY THE JEWS?

Why the Jews? I hear you ask. In order to answer this question, Hannah Arendt tried to understand the situation of the Jews in France after the Dreyfus Affair. The model of France's *fin de siècle* was especially relevant given that, as she wrote, "to a certain extent, what happened in France ... happened thirty and forty years later in all European nation-states." She went back to Proust. In *À la recherche du temps perdu* (*In Search of Lost Time*) she found a subtle account of the way in which the aristocratic salons of the Faubourg Saint-Germain responded to these newcomers. Arendt concluded that French society refused to give up its prejudices. The ruling classes "did not doubt that homosexuals were 'criminals' or that Jews were 'traitors'; they only revised their attitude to crime and treason." Arendt omits to point out that this same society admitted the Jews—while continuing to consider them corrupt—only because it needed their know-how and money. In her view, if it was no longer horrified by the presence of the Jews, it was simply because it was no longer horrified by the crimes it attributed to them.

THE TWO FACETS
OF THE JEWISH
PEOPLE

There is, there were, and there always will be two aspects to the existence of the Jewish people. As in an open book, there is the page on the left and the page on the right: stories and commentaries, Israel and the Diaspora.

It is the same book throughout. There are those who criticize Israel as we would any state whose policies we disapprove. But what is a state? A territory, a people, and a government. In a democracy, there are also opposition forces. Israel has an active opposition and a free press. Criticism of government action from outside will never equal the criticism leveled by local media. But as things stand today, Israel is not a state like other states. It is, as far as I know, the only recognized state whose existence itself is contested, despite its position in the concert of nations. It is not the inhabitants of Israel who claim this exception, but those who want to annihilate them.

So, Israel. Yasser Arafat, he of the kaffiyeh and three-day beard, who for a whole generation of Israelis represented the enemy that must be fought or accommodated, died on November 11, 2004. His old companion, the negotiator of the Oslo Accords, Mahmoud Abbas, replaced him at the head of the Palestinian Authority. In January 2006, he organized the legislative elections called for by the international community. However, these handed a majority to Hamas, a movement that does not recognize the State of Israel and, what's more, features on the list of terrorist organizations. Since the international community was reluctant to officially recognize its victory, Hamas took the Gaza Strip by violence in June 2007. Since then, the two parties in power, the more secular Fatah and the religious Hamas, which is close to the Muslim Brotherhood, have fought over representation of the Palestinians.

*Destroyed buildings
during the Lebanon War
(August 2006, Beirut).*

*"The aim of war is peace"
said Aristotle. Yes, but when?*

In Israel, judging it impossible to settle territorial disputes with the Palestinians by negotiation, the prime minister Ariel Sharon decided to act unilaterally. He evacuated the Jewish inhabitants of Gaza—some of them by force—and returned the territory to the Palestinians. He was about to do the same thing with some of the Jewish colonies in the West Bank when, in January 2006, he suffered a stroke. Ehud Olmert succeeded him at the head of the government. Since he and his foreign minister, Tzipi Livni, lacked Sharon's military prestige, Olmert decided to resume negotiations with the Palestinian Authority. He was nearing an agreement, in particular on the Palestinian presence in Jerusalem, when the Iranians, who have their own strategy in the region, provoked Israel on the battlefield through the intermediary of their protégés, the Lebanese Hezbollah in northern Lebanon and Hamas in Gaza. The Hezbollah attacks on Israeli frontier villages and the abduction of two Tsahal soldiers compelled Israel to react. Hence the Lebanon War of July 2006. The Hezbollah emerged weakened but not defeated, and many died on the Israeli side. Within Tsahal there was criticism of government strategy. Every day, rockets from Gaza showered down on nearby Israeli towns. Hamas abducted the Franco-Israeli soldier Gilad Shalit. This aggression met with an extremely tough Israeli riposte, which some judged disproportionate.

The early legislative elections held in Israel on February 10, 2009, brought Benjamin Netanyahu back to power, his Likud party being supported by others on the Right and by the religious parties. As often in the Near East, the new prime minister forgot the undertakings of his predecessors: all the work had to be done again, or almost all.

POLITICS
SLIPS BACK,
PEOPLE MOVE
AHEAD

But while political leaders always seem to go back to square one, those they represent are moving ahead. Most Israelis accept the idea of a Palestinian state side by side with their own. Of that there is no doubt. For most Palestinians, Israel is a reality and very few of them still dream of driving the Jews into the sea. Some circles are floating the idea of a regional common market encompassing Jordan, Palestine, and Israel, and perhaps—why not?—Syria in the near future. This idea, which is favored by Shimon Peres, is said to be viewed with sympathy by Saudi Arabia. Vying with Iran for the leadership of the Muslim world, Riyadh has everything to gain from pacifying its zone of influence. It has even proposed a global peace between Israel and the Muslim world: a significant step forward.

And what of the Diaspora? We always think first of the big Jewish communities in America, Canada, France, Russia, Britain, and South Africa. It is less usual to mention more modest but nevertheless vigorous communities such as those of Italy, the Netherlands, Belgium, and Australia. And we forget hidden communities, those groups of Jews who have preserved the essence of Judaism when forced to convert to the dominant Christian or Muslim religion. This is the case of the Dönme, which means "turncoats" in Turkish.

Where do they come from? Who are they? I have already mentioned Sabbatai Zevi of Smyrna, the false messiah of the seventeenth century who stirred a great wave of enthusiasm and hope among the millions of wretched Jews in the Orient and Occident. The Ottoman authorities arrested him in September 1666. Fearing for his life, Zevi agreed to convert to Islam and took the name of Aziz Mehmed Efendi. This was a terrible disappointment for the Jewish masses, who had believed in imminent deliverance. In fact, many thought that if he abjured it could only have been on the order of the Eternal One. For what other reason would a messiah convert to Islam?

THE DÖNME

This interpretation was the origin of the Dönme movement. Like their messiah, its members converted to Islam while preserving a number of their practices: they continued to say their prayers in Hebrew, did not marry Muslims, and built their own mosques, where they also read the Psalms in Hebrew. The Dönme had a system of double names: a Turkish name for the outside world and a secret Hebrew name for their family and social group. They were the first to introduce equality between men and women.

At the end of the nineteenth century, many of them espoused the modernist impulse then shaking up Turkish society and joined the secular, nationalist movement of the Young Turks. One of them, Mehmet Cavit Bey, became the finance minister of Mustafa Kemal Atatürk, the founder of modern Turkey. Some have even claimed that Atatürk himself was a Dönme, but without proof. However, Ismail Cem, Turkish foreign minister from 1997 to 2002, did share this faith. Likewise the writers Azra Erhat, Halide Edip Adivar, and Cevat Sakir and the very popular actors Esin Eden and Necdet Mahfi Ayral. How many Dönme are there among the Turkish Muslims? We do not know. Some say a million, others, twenty thousand. We can identify them only in the cemeteries where their tombstones all bear the same inscription: "I hid it; I didn't disclose it; my worries I kept secret until I was laid to rest."

Mustapha Kemal Atatürk with his chiefs of staff (c.1923).

Which of these Young Turks sitting beside Ataturk came from the Dönme?

The Diaspora. And to start with, the biggest Jewish community in the world, that of the United States of America. Not so long ago this was estimated at 5.2 million. However, a very recent study conducted around the country over more than a year by several teams of researchers came up with a figure of 6,443,805—1.2 million more. Here is one striking example: in Jacksonville, Florida, the Jewish Federation previously declared 7,300 members, whereas the new study found 12,900, that is, 5,600 more.

It's the same in Russia: after the massive emigration of the Russian Jews to Israel, the Federation of Jewish Communities now claims 250,000 members. But if we take into account the hundreds of communities in the former Soviet Union, including those of Central Asia, the figure easily rises to one million.

What lies behind this difference? Because censuses based on ethnic criteria are prohibited in democratic countries, statisticians have to make do with the statements provided by Jewish institutions and congregations. However, many Jews today who still consider themselves Jews also say they are secular and do not belong to any community organizations. Then there are mixed couples. For most communities, a Jew married to a non-Jew is lost to Judaism. But Jewish history shows the opposite to be true: there is of course Moses and Zipporah, the black daughter of the Midianite high priest Jethro who, to my knowledge, never converted to Judaism, which did not prevent Moses from achieving what he did. The Bible offers other exemplary mixed couples, starting with Ruth the Moabite and Boaz, the great grandparents of King David. Their love was so great that, according to the writers of the Book, the Messiah will come from their lineage.

Below:
Rembrandt, Boaz Encounters Ruth in His Field *(c.1640, Musée du Louvre, Paris).*

Facing page:
Marc Chagall, Meeting of Ruth and Boaz *(1960, Musée National Marc Chagall, Nice).*

This is the most famous mixed couple in Jewish history: the great grandparents of King David.

Marc Chagall

As for converts, despite the resistance of the rabbis, there have been many, and some have played a key role in Jewish history. Hillel the Babylonian became the head of a rabbinic school in the late first century BCE; Akiva, a Greek converted to Judaism at the age of forty, made an eminent contribution to the composition of the Talmud and was the spiritual leader of the last revolt against Rome in 132 CE.

If we set the number of Jews living in the Diaspora today alongside the population of Israel, we find that we have two coherent blocs, much as there were in the biblical era. Even if the 7,951,250 Jews of the Diaspora do outnumber the Jews living in Israel by a million.

In 586 BCE, before the Babylonian king Nebuchadnezzar destroyed the Temple, there were as many Jews in Jerusalem as there were in Alexandria. Today, more than 2,600 years later, there are comparable numbers of Jews living in Tel Aviv and in New York: 2,799,000 for Tel Aviv and 2,151,000 for New York. On one side, a community rooted in the land of its ancestors; on the other, communities rooted in the Book, going where history leads, from one city to another: Babylon, Rome, Cordoba, Kairouan, Troyes, Baghdad, Worms, Warsaw.

At the birth of the State of Israel, David Ben Gurion was concerned that the spirit of *Golah* (exile in Hebrew) would overcome the new country. He therefore banned the teaching of Yiddish and Judeo-Spanish in schools. He hoped that Israeli youth would rediscover the values and virtues of their ancestors, the Maccabees. Language, the old and the new Hebrew, played a central role in the renaissance of the Hebrew nation. In the 1950s the Canaanist movement, supported by the journalist Uri Avnery and the writer Amos Kenan, set out to reconquer not only the land but also the past. Many Sabras (Jews born in Israel) made it a point of honor to speak the kind of guttural Hebrew spoken by the prophets at the time of the Temple. They sang only Hebraic songs, they read only Haim Nahman Bialik, Shmuel Yosef Agnon (Nobel Prize for Literature, 1966), and Haim Hazaz, and they recited only the fervid, nationalist poems of Uri Zvi Greenberg. For them, the Diaspora boiled down to a tragic past punctuated by pogroms that culminated in the ovens of Auschwitz.

Facing page, left:
Arrests during the Warsaw Ghetto Uprising (April–May 1943).

Facing page, right:
Werner Braun, Eichmann during his trial in Jerusalem (1961).

With the Eichmann trial a whole generation of Sabras, or Jews born in Israel, learned about the machine that destroyed their brothers, but also their brothers' bravery.

The great shock came in 1961 with the Eichmann trial. It was held in Jerusalem and was public. The Israelis discovered not only the infernal machine invented by the Nazis that destroyed their families in Europe, but also the heroism and abnegation of those millions of Jews, their brothers. They learned that the Jews of the Diaspora did not give themselves up to their killers without a struggle, that armed uprisings even in the death camps of Sobibor, Treblinka, and Auschwitz compelled the admiration of the non-Jewish world. They became interested in postwar Jewish writers in the United States, France, the United Kingdom, or Italy.

They understood that, whatever the quality of their literature, their cinema, and their art, the books, films, and paintings of the Diaspora had a serious advance, even if their work was inspired by Israel's growing status. The land is one source of creation but, it must be admitted, books are even more conducive to the writing of books. This can already be seen with the Talmud in the fifth century CE. It is no coincidence that the Diaspora preferred the Babylonian Talmud, written in Hebrew and Aramaic, to the Jerusalem Talmud. It is richer and more detailed. Closer to our own time, when the Israeli writer Shmuel Yosef Agnon won the Nobel Prize for Literature in 1966, he shared it with the German-speaking Jewish poet Nelly Sachs: as if to maintain the balance between Israel and the Diaspora.

THE EICHMANN TRIAL

209

The Diaspora needs Israel in order to survive: as a dream or, better, as a reality. Israel needs the Diaspora, for there it can stay connected to the universal. The distinctive position of the Diaspora, scattered among nations, rests on its double roots, in national cultures and in its own ancestral memory: more fragile than Israel when caught in the storms of history, it is artistically more productive. When they hear of "danger," the Jews of Israel get out their weapons; the Jews of the Diaspora reach for their culture.

As if to ensure the continuous chain of Jewish creativity, during his early career Saul Bellow, winner of the Nobel Prize for Literature in 1976, translated short stories by Isaac Bashevis Singer—who won the same prize in 1978—from Yiddish into English. In the same way Bernard Malamud and Chaim Potok, Henry Roth, Arthur Miller, Herman Wouk, Allen Ginsberg, Norman Mailer, and Philip Roth began by looking at the world of their parents, that world of yesterday to which Woody Allen is always paying homage. Most American Jews remain attached to Israel, even if two-thirds of them have never been there.

Below, left:
Franz Kafka (c.1907).

Below, right:
*Romain Gary
in Rome (1962).*

Facing page, left:
Primo Levi.

Facing page, right:
Woody Allen (1980).

*It is not enough to
remember: one must also
pass on the memory.*

In short, it would not be chauvinistic to marvel at the tremendous creative dynamism of the Diaspora Jews. We know about Jewish literary output in the German language: Stefan Zweig, Arthur Schnitzler, Hermann Broch, Jakob Wassermann, Alfred Döblin, Max Brod, Franz Kafka, and many more, not forgetting figures such as Sigmund Freud, Edmund Husserl, and Hannah Arendt. We are maybe less familiar with Jewish literature in Italian: Primo Levi, Carlo Levi, Giorgio Bassani, Natalia Ginzburg, Umberto Saba, Italo Svevo, and Alberto Moravia, who said he was Jewish through his father Pincherle. And then, of course, there are the contemporary Jewish writers in French—Albert Cohen, Emmanuel Berl, Romain Gary, Georges Perec, André Schwarz-Bart, Patrick Modiano—and the philosophers Claude Lévi-Strauss, Emmanuel Levinas, Jacques Derrida, Raymond Aron, Vladimir Jankélévitch, Bernard-Henri Lévy, Alain Finkielkraut, and André Glucksmann.

A Lesson at
the Heder, *Lublin*
(c. 1920, BPK, Berlin).

*"The world only exists because
of the breath of small children
studying the Torah." (Babylon
Talmud, Shabbat, 119 b).*

The Ethics of the Fathers says:

> Moses received the Torah at Sinai and handed it down to
> Joshua, and Joshua to the Elders, and the Elders to the
> Prophets; and the Prophets handed it down to the men of
> the Great Assembly. They [the Men of the Great Assembly]
> would always say these three things: "Be cautious in
> judgment. Establish many pupils. And make a safety fence
> around the Torah.

Jewish history teaches us that it is not enough to assemble human
wisdom in books and study it; one must hand it on. Assiduous study
itself becomes a means of transmission: the one who transmits learns,
the one who learns transmits. The two are inseparable. Together they
create the People of the Book, a people of questioning and memory,
a people of the Law and of answers. It is in the dialectical subtlety of
study that the Jews scattered around the world have found the only
way of reconstructing a social link destroyed by the separation of
individuals. Even today, the unity of the Jewish people, combining
Israel and the Diaspora, is thoroughly interwoven with texts and
men's relation to them, however much this may fluctuate.

Religious Jews consider that the original word is that of the
Eternal One and that the texts engraved by Moses were dictated to
him by God. To attempt to fully grasp their meaning, to decipher
their hidden intentions, and hear their silences—this, for them,
remains the surest way of approaching God. The secular Jew may
have lost this deep relation to the Text, but he has kept its practices
and customs. He practices an art of reading, an attention to the word,
to what is written, that give his thought a very particular cast which
some consider specifically Jewish. Popular jokes make much of this
curious exploration of the letter of the Text, this constant search for a
pretext for thinking.

A thought must be handled like material at once soft and unyielding.
It requires constant effort, a dialogue with the other. "Choose
yourself a master, get yourself a study companion," says the Ethics of
the Fathers. We construct our intellectual life with our fellows. This
obliges us, says Jewish wisdom, to take an interest in the community,
to open ourselves to the world, to hear the other's voice. Voice and
gaze: are Jews Jews primarily, as Jean-Paul Sartre said, in the eyes of
the anti-Semite?

"CHOOSE YOURSELF
A MASTER,
GET YOURSELF
A STUDY COMPANION"

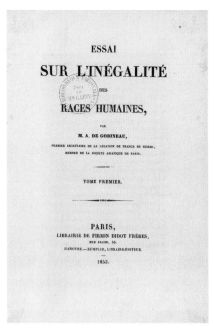

ANTI-ZIONISM:
ANTI-JUDAISM?

W hich brings us back to anti-Semitism. According to all the recent studies, classical anti-Semitism, the kind that comes to us from Apion in antiquity, via Gobineau, Maurras, and Bloy, is receding. According to the report by the Anti-Defamation League, anti-Jewish aggression in the United States has decreased recently by over 22 percent. This is also the case, if sometimes to a lesser degree, in other countries. In a civilization still marked by the Holocaust, it takes some doing to shout out "dirty Jew!"

In France, for example, a recent survey shows that 90 percent of the population considers the French Jews as normal fellow citizens. But if we look more closely, we will see that Judeophobia itself has not diminished. It seems simply to have changed its target. It is not Jews that are targeted but Israel. Anti-Judaism has been transformed into anti-Zionism, and since Israel is a Jewish state, all Jews are tainted by its "faults."

In a report commissioned in 2004 by the French government, the writer Jean-Christophe Rufin speaks of a "more heterogeneous anti-Semitism." He observes the emergence of a new kind of anti-Judaism, "radical anti-Zionism," which is developing not on the old Right, but on the extreme Left and in anti-globalization movements. Their aim is to legitimize the armed struggle of the Palestinians against Israel.

On September 9, 2001, the United Nations organized a conference on racism in Durban, South Africa. The result was to unleash a wave of Judeophobia and Holocaust-denying, under the mask of anti-Zionism. Copies of *Mein Kampf* were handed out, along with *The Protocols of the Elders of Zion*. After an interminable speech by Fidel Castro, where the crowd was whipped up into hysteria, there were calls to kill the Jews. The hatred was not aimed at the policies of the Israeli government, but at Israel itself and, above all—quite simply—at the Jews. The South African police struggled to protect the city's one synagogue against the wild crowd. Participants not wearing the kaffiyeh were dismissed as "Jewish Pig Lovers." Seeing this pogrom-like frenzy at an event organized by the so-called "human rights" commission of the United Nations, even a man as moderate as Kofi Annan, then secretary-general of the organization, said that he was "horrified."

In 2009 I managed to get into Gaza with a Convoy for Peace. Also there were the imam of Drancy in France, Hassen Chalghoumi, and the rabbi of Ris-Orangis, Michel Serfaty, the first rabbi to set foot in this Palestinian enclave controlled by the extremist group Hamas. When the rabbi got back to Marseille, young French men of North African origin shouted out, "You're a good Jew." "Why?" asked the rabbi. "Are there bad Jews?" "Yes, the Zionists." "Do you know what Zion means?" asked the rabbi. "Yes, *The Protocols of the Elders of Zion*." They had no idea that it was a false document fabricated by the Czar's police just before the Revolution. Today, this text which brings together all the hoary old anti-Jewish arguments has become the handbook of anti-Semitism.

In the verbal campaign conducted against Israel, in some cases by sincere supporters of the Palestinian cause, it is rare for the Koran to be quoted. Why? Because these people haven't read it. They therefore get their arguments from the hoary repertoire of Western anti-Semitism. Louis Farrakhan in the United States, for example, accuses the Jews of having dragged America into the war against Iraq and having bought up the whole of Hollywood. Even the torturers of the young Ilan Halimi, who was killed in France in 2006 because he was a Jew, justified themselves with anti-Zionist slogans.

Accused by the British press of making anti-Semitic statements, the mayor of London, Ken Livingstone, replied that he was not an anti-Semite, simply an anti-Zionist. In March 2009, that year's edition of Turin's annual International Book Fair, the biggest of its kind in Italy, organized a homage to Israeli literature and its great writers, such as Amos Oz, A. B. Yehoshua, David Grossman, Aharon Appelfeld, and many more. But, in order to punish them for the policies of their government, several Italian writers and philosophers such as Edoardo Sanguineti, Gianni Vattimo, and Dario Fo, winner of the Nobel Prize for Literature, called for a boycott of the Israeli writers. Encouraged by this campaign, another petition also circulated at University of Rome: quite simply, it called for the exclusion of professors of Jewish origin for the crime of Zionism. Anti-Judaism has changed its name, but we would be wrong to ignore it.

As the Jews know, life in a community, with the sharing of ideas and the cohabitation of cultures, is not always a bed of roses. The life of thought can often threaten to turn into conflict leading, ultimately, to rejection. That is when one must come back to the source of this living thought and rediscover its purposes and its function in the spirit of the Law, which always seeks union. In other words, in the spirit of Judaism, the study of texts and the development of understanding are man's vital guides and the free enrichment of his identity.

This spiraling movement, which never goes in circles, returns to the same point, and is always developing because of new thoughts, new encounters, and new wisdom, is what characterizes the Jewish spirit.

It was Nietzsche, wrongly accused of anti-Semitism after his death, who most clearly understood the subversive side of the Jewish people, and therefore one of the causes of its repeated persecution:

WITH THE JEWS BEGINS THE SLAVE INSURRECTION

> The Jews—a people "born into slavery," according to Tacitus and the whole ancient world—the Jews brought about that tour de force of a reversal of values that enabled life on earth to acquire a new and dangerous charm for one or two thousand years. Their prophets fused "rich," "godless," "evil," "violent." ... In this reversal of values (part of which is to treat the word "poor" as a synonym for "saint" and "friend") lies the significance of the Jewish people: the *slave revolt in morals begins* with them. (Friedrich Nietzsche, *Beyond Good and Evil*, 1886.)

Gustave Doré, Moses Shatters the Tablets of the Law, *illustration for the Tours Bible (1866).*

From Moses to the present day, history can be summed up as the long process of learning to be free, of the slow emancipation from idols.

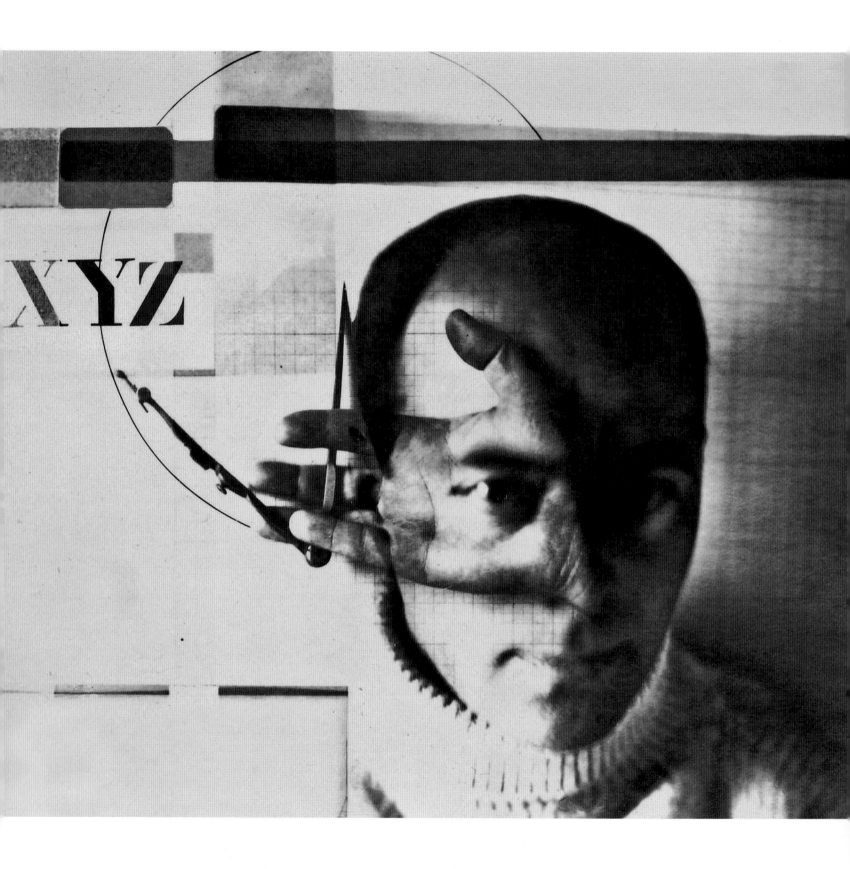

Rabbi Enoch says: "Israel's true exile began in Egypt, with learning to endure it." Why this judgment? The rabbi observes that the exiles submitted; they accepted the yoke on their shoulders. They did not defend the freedom that God had entrusted to them: they sinned. One must break free of slavery, not only because it makes men suffer, but also because it is contrary to the Law. Slavery is a manifestation of evil. To learn to endure it is to take the evil *into oneself*, at the risk of reproducing it in turn.

It is not enough to break the chain around one's ankle and run away. Even far away, even in the desert. The slave can free himself from the power of evil only through consciousness of evil, the evil that is slavery passed on like an infection. Thus and only thus will he become a man free of *all* slavery.

Rabbi Enoch's words explain very well what happened in Iran. After the long monarchic dictatorship, Ayatollah Khomeini led the Iranian people along the path of revolt and overturned the shah. Immediately, we saw this liberated people enthusiastically throw itself into a new slavery, even harder than the one they had just shattered. Clearly, the Iranian people did not have a clear awareness of this evil when they threw it off. For, beyond the causes and responsibilities of slavery, there are also the reasons why one accepts it, submits to it, or reproduces it. That is the root, which one must know in order to tear it up.

To pass on the original Text and to interpret it: that is the commentator's task. To cultivate memory and nourish it with the facts of life, from the most extraordinary to the most elementary: such was and such still is the fundamental task of a people that was the first to realize that man was caught up in history.

What could be nobler than trying to better understand the Text, and then the texts on the Text, the story of the stories? Probing, analyzing, and producing commentary on them? This twofold movement toward the depth and toward the light of life in the present is what singularizes and identifies the Jewish reader. Ever since the first Text, he has constantly enriched our libraries with magnificent works that—right up until modern times—have enlivened not only Jewish thought but that of all humanity.

In 1575 Joseph ha-Kohen, a Jewish doctor in Avignon, completed the writing of his *The Vale of Tears*, relating the sufferings of Israel and the Diaspora over the centuries. After him came another witness, an anonymous man this time, who continued the work. In his introduction, he writes these deeply moving words which sum up my own life today:

Lazar Lissitzky, Self-portrait with Compass (1924, Kupferstich-Kabinett, national collection, Dresden).

Cultivating memory, the "warder of the brain" as Shakespeare wrote.

"I have resolved to set down in this book everything that has happened to the Jews since that other Joseph ended his chronicle and up to the present time, in order to fulfill the precept: 'That you may tell it to the ears of your son and your grandson.'"

JUDAISM: SUBVERSIVE THOUGHT

The concern is always the same: to pass on, to communicate and share, and, finally, to teach. The Jewish-German poet Heinrich Heine called this "the plague that Judaism brought back from the valley of the Nile." I myself would call it "subversive thought."

If, for the Greeks and Romans, civil virtues "concern only free men," such a distinction is inconceivable for Judaism. For the Jews, every son of Israel has a predisposition for freedom. But can one be free in a world that is not? That is why, having only just been freed from slavery themselves, Jews called for universal liberation in their texts. However, they can call for it only insofar as they are Jews. If they lose their particular memory, they lose their desire for liberation; if they lose their desire for liberation, they cease to be Jews. We can see what a danger Jews represent for totalitarian systems and ideologies, and why, without exception, such regimes persecute and try to annihilate them.

THE GUARDIANS OF THE BOOK

In *Nineteen Eighty-Four*, a novel published in 1948, George Orwell offers a unique description of the totalitarian system, in which men are crushed by the all-seeing gaze of the tyrant, a Stalin figure called Big Brother. Among the millions of individuals who accept the unacceptable, only one escapes: Emmanuel Goldstein. It is surely no coincidence that Orwell named him thus, and that, as the owner and presumed author of "the book," "a compendium of all the heresies," Goldstein should be the despot's number-one target. In a world where books are deemed subversive and inspire hatred, the man who has preserved the idea of freedom symbolized by a book represents both the beginning and the end of history: the guarantee of its continuity.

Coming to the end of this *Jewish Odyssey*, I wonder if it does not sum up the story of Goldstein; or if Goldstein, this character imagined by Orwell in the aftermath of World War II, might not embody the odyssey of the Jewish people: keeper of the book, a mission that is burningly clear, but also, as we know, beset with danger.

Ezra (miniature from the Codex Amiantino, fifth century BCE, *Laurentian Library, Florence).*

Ever since Ezra (fifth century BCE) *the Jews have been rooted in the Book.*

BIBLIOGRAPHY

- Arendt, Hannah. "The Jews as Pariah" and "Between Vice and Crime" in *Reflections on Literature and Culture*. Edited by Susannah Young-ah Gottlieb. Palo Alto: Stanford University Press, 2007.

- Aron, Raymond. *De Gaulle, Israel and the Jews*. Translated by John Sturrock. London: André Deutsch, 1969.

- Barnavi, Eli. *A Historical Atlas of the Jewish People, from the Time of the Patriarchs to the Present*. New York: Schocken Books, 2003.

- Baron, Salo. *Ancient and Mediaeval Jewish History*. Newark: Rutgers University Press, 1986.

- Bashevis Singer, Isaac. *Gimpel the Fool and Other Stories*. Translated by Saul Bellow. New York: Farrar, Straus and Giroux, 2006.

- Berg, Rav. *The Essential Zohar: The Source of Kabbalistic Wisdom*. New York: Random House: 2002.

- Bergson, Henri. *Laughter: An Essay on the Meaning of the Comic*. Translated by Cloudesley Brereton and Fred Rothwell. Mineola: Dover Publications, 2005.

- Buck, Pearl. *Peony*. New York: John Day, 1948.

- Chateaubriand, René François. *Travels in Greece, Palestine, Egypt, and Barbary, During the Years 1806 and 1807*. Translated by Frederic Shoberl. New York: Van Winkle and Wiley, 1841.

- Dubnow, Simon. *History of the Jews in Russia and Poland*. Philadelphia: The Jewish Publication Society of America, 1916–20.

- Dunn, James David. *Window of the Soul: The Kabbalah of Rabbi Isaac Luria*. Newburyport: Weiser Books, 2008.

- Freud, Sigmund. *Jokes and Their Relation to the Unconscious*. Edited by James Strachey and Peter Gay. New York: W.W. Norton & Company, 1990.

- Goldberg, Sylvie Anne. *Dictionnaire encyclopédique du judaïsme*. Paris: Robert Laffont, Bouquins, 1996.

- Ha-Kohen, Joseph. *The Vale of Tears*. Translated by Harry May. The Hague: Martinus Nijhoff, 1971.

- Halevi, Judah. *The Kuzari: An Argument for the Faith of Israel*. New York: Random House, 1964.

- Halter, Marek. *The Book of Abraham*. Boston: H. Holt, 1983.

- ——. *The Messiah*. Translated by Lauren Yoder. New York / London: The Toby Press, 2008.

- ——. *Zipporah, Wife of Moses*. Translated by Howard Curtis. New York: Crown Publishers, Random House, 2006.

- Herzl, Theodor. *A Jewish State: An Attempt at a Modern Solution of the Jewish Question*. Translated by I.M. Lask. London: Penguin Classic, 2010.

- Hochhuth, Rolf. *The Deputy*. Translated by Richard and Clara Winston. New York: Grove Press, 1964.

- Josephus, Flavius. *The War of the Jews*. Translated by Dean Aldrich. Charlotte: IAP, 2009.

- ——. *Against Apion*. Translated by William Whiston. Wilder Publications, 2009.

- Kafka, Franz. *The Diaries of Franz Kafka*. Edited by Max Brod. New York: Schocken Books, 1988.

- Levi, Primo. *If This Is a Man*. Translated by S. Woolf. New York: The Orion Press, 1969.

- Luther, Martin. "That Jesus Christ was Born a Jew" in *Luther's Works*. Philadelphia: Fortress Press, 1962.

- Maimon, Salomon. *Autobiography*. Translated by J. Clark Murray. Champaign: University of Illinois Press, 2001.

- Nietzsche, Friedrich. *Beyond Good and Evil*. Translated by R. J. Hollingdale. London: Penguin Classics, 2003.

- Orwell, George. *Nineteen Eighty-Four*. London: Secker and Warburg, 1949.

- Philo of Alexandria. "On the Embassy to Gaius" in *The Works of Philo*. Translated by Charles Duke Yonge. Peabody: Hendrickson Publishers, 1993.

- Proust, Marcel. *In Search of Lost Time*. Translated by Terence Kilmartin, D.J. Enright, and C.K.Scott Moncrieff. London: Vintage, 1996.

- Rawicz, Piotr. *Blood from the Sky*. Translated by Peter Wiles. New Haven: Yale University Press, 2003.

- Ringelblum, Emmanuel. *Notes from the Warsaw Ghetto*. Translated by Jacob Sloan. New York: Schocken Books, 1974.

- Wansbrough, Henry (ed). *The New Jerusalem Bible*. London: Darton, Longman & Todd Ltd, 1960.

- Werblowsky, R.J. Zwri and Geoffrey Wigoder (eds). *The Oxford Dictionary of the Jewish Religion*. Oxford: OUP, 1997.

- Wiesel, Elie. *The Jews of Silence*. Translated by Neal Kozodoy. New York: Holt, Rinehart and Winston, 1966.

INDEX

The page numbers in bold refer to illustrations.